MARY WEBB: COLLECTED PROSE AND POEMS

Other books by Gladys Mary Coles:

THE FLOWER OF LIGHT: A BIOGRAPHY OF MARY WEBB

MARY WEBB: SELECTED POEMS
(edited, with an Introduction)

THE SOUNDING CIRCLE AND OTHER POEMS

SINERVA AND OTHER POEMS

MARY WEBB
Collected Prose and Poems

A Selection
of Mary Webb's hitherto Uncollected and Unpublished Work

Edited with an Introduction by
GLADYS MARY COLES

Published by
WILDINGS OF SHREWSBURY LTD.

To

LYNNE AND KATHRYN

for "growing up" with M.W.

ISBN 0 85489 015 7

© Gladys Mary Coles 1977: this Selection, Introduction and Editorial Arrangement
© the Executors of the Mary Webb Estate 1977

Printed and Published by
WILDINGS OF SHREWSBURY LTD., WINDSOR PLACE, SHREWSBURY, SY1 2DB

CONTENTS

POEMS

INTRODUCTION

. . . Like a bird, with wings
Dusky and silent, I would flit through spring's
Wistful, immaculate colours.

During the nineteen-twenties a small, frail-looking woman with large, brilliant, anxious eyes would frequently be seen in Shrewsbury station. Dressed in dark, untidy clothes and clutching a little case which contained her manuscripts, she would descend from the London train, come into the station yard beneath the castle, and take a cab out of the town to Lyth Hill. Once there in her own cottage and garden, she would work at her writing, tend her flowers, sit at the edge of the wooded plateau, drinking in with her eyes and soul the view across 'the enchanted plain' to the 'blue ring of hills.' For Mary Webb, this was her 'home of colour and light'—a haven for her spirit—far removed from the sad, distressing sights in post-war London, the beggars she tried to help, the literary world which had disappointed her.

On October 8th, 1927, at the age of forty-six, she died of Graves' Disease (exopthalmic goitre) and pernicious anaemia. In an intensely creative life, the final twelve years had been a concentrated period of literary effort during which she produced six novels (one uncompleted), numerous poems, short stories, essays and reviews. But the public had remained indifferent to her work, though *Gone To Earth* was proclaimed 'novel of the year' in 1917, *Precious Bane* won the Prix Femina Vie Heureuse for 1924, and her reputation was high in more exclusive literary and publishing circles. She died without popular success, worn out by struggle and deep personal distress. The following April when the spring grass was growing on her grave, the birds singing and rounding their nests in her garden at Lyth Hill, people everywhere were in search of her novels, some of which (including *Gone To Earth*) were out of print: Baldwin's tribute to Mary Webb at the Royal Literary Fund dinner was having considerable public reverberation, and had brought her posthumous fame, literally overnight. To meet the enormous demand, Jonathan Cape brought out the Collected Edition of her works, with Introductions by well known literary figures (and by Baldwin himself to the now best-selling *Precious Bane*). An ironical story.

We sing our song in beauty's fading tree,
And flash forth, migrant, into mystery.

*

When the final volume of Mary Webb's posthumous Collected Works was published, a *Times* critic commented that 'Lovers of her work . . . will welcome these last crumbs which have all the flavour of her best loaves.' This was early in 1929. Now, almost half a century later, we have an entirely new Mary Webb volume, consisting of previously uncollected and unpublished writings, and presenting a little known aspect of her literary achievement.

During the research for my biography of Mary Webb, *The Flower Of Light*, I set out to find all her ephemera, the scattered writings which I was sure existed. These were garnered from various sources, some so obscure and remote that I would never have traced them but for an extraordinary combination of intuition, good fortune and naive perseverance; others were discovered after many back-aching but fascinating hours searching the literary journals, periodicals and newspapers of her day. I was rewarded by the exhilaration of finding a quantity of Mary Webb material confirming my conviction that her literary output was far greater than had previously been thought.

These 'discoveries' have obviously been of inherent value in my study of her life and work; subsequently I decided to assemble the best of them in book form, making permanent and readily available to the reading public writings which would otherwise be lost in periodicals (some long since expired). It seemed appropriate to present a selection of these Mary Webb pieces to mark the fiftieth anniversary year of her death (1977), and particularly appropriate to publish them in her native Shropshire which had been essential to her life and art.

This new volume of her work should prove of great interest not only to those who already know and appreciate her writing, but also to students and to the new readers whom, I hope, it will attract. Her prose pieces have intrinsic merit, and remind us again of Walter de la Mare's words: 'few writers indeed have left behind them so rich a posthumous gift.' And the volume is timely in view of the revival of interest in her work: Mary Webb is a writer whose relevance is likely to increase, especially as the taste in fiction is changing in a renascence of romantic literature rooted in universal myth and folktale.

The present collection is not merely miscellaneous pieces brought together in an anthology. Giving coherence and unity to the whole is, of course, the highly individual voice and vision of Mary Webb; we find on every page, whether in early poems or in last review articles, the artistic integrity, the essential qualities and concerns which inform her major works, the novels. Mary Webb's entire literary output is the varied expression of her unique personal vision: so her total work has cohesion, the lesser writings, articles, reviews, short stories and earlier poems standing in significant relation to the main body of novels and mature poems. It remains true, however, that her finest achievement lies in her novels with their Shropshire settings and rich, haunting sense of place. These are kept in print by her publisher, Jonathan Cape.

In this volume, the creative and critical writings extend over almost every phase of Mary's literary life: in particular, they expand our knowledge of her early work as a poet and her later work as a reviewer and critic. Some belong to the years when she was still immersed in her blissful childhood environment of a cultured 'country house' home in Shropshire with her adored father at the centre of the Meredith family circle. But the greater part of them belong to the last period of her life—the six years she spent between London and Shropshire when, at times, she had barely enough cash to buy food and was seeking quick returns from articles and stories, though frequently on receiving a cheque she spent the money on destitutes instead of paying bills. Then faced by mounting debts she felt, as she told Jonathan Cape in a letter, 'like an ant under a landslip.' Often she urgently needed money to buy rail tickets to Shrewsbury, her yearning for her countryside becoming increasingly intense, her migrations back and forth more frequent.

I have arranged the writings in three sections as they hold together naturally. The first is 'Short Stories'. In 1928 ten of her stories (some little more than sketches), were hastily gathered and published with the unfinished novel, *Armour Wherein He Trusted*. These stories, as Martin Armstrong said in his Introduction, 'are of unequal merit' and 'seldom if ever reach the level of her novels and poems.' But the five previously uncollected stories I have included here constitute a stronger group and demonstrate more effectively her gift as a teller of tales. J. B. Priestley once said that a short story 'can give us two things, a point (or a situation) and a manner (or an atmosphere), and a really good one will give us both.' The art is primarily one of compression, of distillation and selection from experience; because of the smallness of the short story we can envisage it as a whole, take it like a crystal glass, study its design, its light and shade, its completeness. In the best of her stories, Mary Webb gives us this satisfaction by her accomplished command, her always fresh and arresting perceptions, her feeling for the magic of words.

The appeal of her earliest published story, 'A Cedar-Rose', which first appeared in *Country Life* (1909), is in the gentle lyricism of its telling. Here already we find that lucidity of style and use of symbolism so characteristic of her novels. The other stories I have selected were written in the final years when, migrant between London and Shropshire, she was declining physically, yet trying desperately hard to place the shorter writings she was producing when not working at her novels. 'Mr. Tallent's Ghost' is an intriguing parable told with wit and verve. It has a fine opening manner and is compelling from start to finish. 'The Cuckoo Clock'—for children of all ages—is an amusing fable imbued with rather sinister overtones. This story is invested with her typically sharp descriptive power, humorous observation and imaginative energy. Both of these stories were accepted by Lady Cynthia Asquith for collections she was compiling: Mr. Tallent's Ghost in *The Ghost Book* (1926) which included tales by D. H. Lawrence, Walter de la Mare, Hugh Walpole, Algernon Blackwood and other well known writers; 'The Cuckoo Clock' in *Sails Of Gold*, published in October 1927, soon after Mary's death.

Two love stories, 'The Sword' and *The Chinese Lion*, are bathed in the Twenties atmosphere. These (together with 'Mr. Tallent's Ghost'), mark a departure from her usual countryside settings and characters—city stories, more sophisticated in tone, they were not published during Mary's life, but after she died they were found among her papers by her husband, Henry B. L. Webb, who later arranged for their publication. 'The Sword' first appeared in *The Cornhill Magazine* in 1934, and *The Chinese Lion* was published by Bertram Rota in 1937.

'Glimpses of Old Shropshire' was specially written by Mary Webb as a paper for the Caradoc and Severn Valley Field Club: it was read to the members at a meeting on March 16th 1923, but 'Mrs. Webb greatly regretted that she could not be present herself to read the paper.' Subsequently published in the Field Club *Transactions* and the *Shrewsbury Chronicle*, it consists of two vivid pieces of historical writing, a glimpse into lost realities, based on careful and accurate research. 'The Return of the Romans: A Dream of Uriconium' is an evocation of Roman Shropshire and the once thriving, extensive city at Wroxeter. This describes the journey of a Roman centurion, his soldiers and convoy of bullock carts returning in early autumn from the lead mines at Snailbeach over the Stiperstones and across Lyth Hill to Viroconium, 'the only town in that lone countryside,' which gleams where 'its roofs of glittering spar catch the lovely western light of afternoon.' Mary Webb, born not far from the Roman city, at the village of Leighton (under the Wrekin), was fascinated, like Wilfred Owen, by this 'grassy town' with its ruined walls, and wrote of it again in one of her finest poems. Excavations of the site were much in the news in 1923 as the pre-war work (abandoned in 1914) was resumed. In the second part of her paper, Mary brings before us a medieval scene, depicting 'Shrewsbury's Abbey Fair' at the time of its founding by Roger de Montgomery in the eleventh century. She had, as one critic said, 'an imagination that broke down barriers: barriers of the spirit and barriers of time.' Hers was a mind saturated in the moods and atmosphere of her county, and in its past, ever present. 'Glimpses of Old Shropshire' with its imaginative penetration into the past, indicates the direction her work took in her last two novels, both set in the Shropshire of earlier times. With consummate artistry she made 'the lapse of centuries seem of little moment.'

The second section, 'Essays, Articles, Reviews', reveals an important though lesser known area of Mary Webb's literary achievement. Here in her work as a reviewer and critic, we find her most direct utterance. These pages are permeated with her personality.

It was late in 1922, with four novels and a book of nature essays published, that she was first engaged as a book reviewer (although she had some early experience with the *Liverpool Post*). Mary wanted 'to write for the reviews' partly to further her name as she was eager to capture a wider public, and partly to earn money. Such 'bread and butter work' was greatly sought after by writers in the post-war period of depression leading to the General Strike of 1926. It was a mark of Mary Webb's growing reputation that she was offered regular reviewing (signed contributions) by two leading periodicals—*The Spectator* and *The Bookman*. The literary editors of these were themselves influential critics, and gave Mary 'some reviewing' not because 'she looked pathetic or pestered them for work, but for the reason that they saw in her a great artist'—the words are those of Caradoc Evans, the Welsh writer, who thought highly of her novels and invited her to contribute articles to *T.P's and Cassell's Weekly*, of which he was Assistant Editor.

Between December 1922 and September 1927, Mary wrote approximataly one review a month, pressured by necessity and deadlines, expending thought, time and energy she might otherwise have given to her imaginative literature: as she confided to Ellery Sedgwick, a literary American (editor of *Atlantic Monthly*), she found it 'hard to trade words for bread.' Nevertheless, she gave deep consideration to the books under review, taking her responsibilities very seriously since she herself as a novelist felt it keenly when reviewers treated her work cursorily or 'did not see what she was doing.' As St. John Adcock, *The Bookman* editor, pointed out, Mary was 'an acute and discerning critic, and wrote her reviews with all the care and grace of fancy and beauty of phrase she put into her novels.' She tended to worry a great deal about her work—occasional writings as much as novels. Caradoc Evans recalled how she came on the phone repeatedly after sending him 'The Poetry of the Prayer Book', wanting to change words and phrases, even phoning the printer until told that the issue had 'gone to bed.'

And certainly, in trading words for bread, she left us a feast. Her reviews—lively, interesting, perceptive, salted with wit—reveal everywhere her acute sensibility, the integrity of her opinions: 'it was clear,' said Frank Swinnerton, 'that she knew her own mind and would hold it in spite of any other opinion.' Bearing her unique imprint, the reviews add immensely to our knowledge of her as a person and a writer. Reading them, we have a sense of immediate contact as if listening to her across the table for two in her tiny Hampstead cottage where she sat at the flower-filled window, a slight, fragile figure yet eager and intense, looking out to the minute garden with its one lime tree.

In December 1922, Mary began writing regularly for *The Spectator* and contributed until late June 1925. The literary editor, Martin Armstrong, admired in her novels 'the richness and intensity of her description of the natural scene' . . . 'the sharp and delicate style of so much of her writing'. Especially impressed by her intimate knowledge of nature, he engaged her to review natural history books, children's nature books and novels of country life (then increasingly popular). She had a specialist's task, reviewing books by distinguished authorities such as Henri Fabre. In these reviews the range and detail of her knowledge is revealed, and not just of bees, birds, beasts and flowers, as she often breaks through the imposed limits of this form of writing to express her own preoccupations and ideas—for instance, her antipathy to bloodsports, her views on the influence of the subconscious, instinct and intuition, questions which delve 'to the heart of creation.' And like Edward Thomas in his reviews, she indulges now and then in lyrical digressions, though occasionally apologising for 'the enormity of such disquisitions.' Reading nature books and writing about them reminded her of Shropshire and relieved the dreariness of London which she regarded as 'a desert.' Yet while she was transported to her fields, hills, woods—a recaptured world—at the same time this intensified her *hiraeth*, clearly reflected in the reviews.

For Mary Webb the physical world was 'almost intolerably lovely' and her spiritual response to it was that of a mystic. But there was nothing indefinite or hazy in her attitude, and as a naturalist endowed with the keenest of senses, she looked for precision in the nature books she was reviewing. Nothing less than accuracy will do when nature is the subject. Not hesitating to point out mistakes (particularly critical of illustrations to bird books), she is generous in her praise of exactitude, admiring a writer who 'says exactly what he saw, and the plainer the writing, the more rapture his memories bring to the reader. Only the true naturalist dares to be terse and simple.' She herself, as the reviews show, had 'the sure touch of the lover of earth who not only loves but knows.' Neither was there anything sentimental in her attitude: she stresses nature's indifference to man, and tells us in a typically aphoristic comment, 'It is as unwise to be sentimental towards Nature as it would be to sonnetize in her presence the rosy lips of a cannibal queen.'

In June 1925, Mary ceased writing for *The Spectator*, as she was engaged to review literature for *The Bookman*. Her aptitude for literary criticism is seen in these *Bookman* reviews and short essays on authors, some well known, some now forgotten. Written when she was reaching her prime as a literary artist, they well bear out the statement in her belated *Times* obituary that 'she was probably at her death on the verge of making a great reputation.' Mary's approach here is that of a novelist not that of the 'common reader' (to use Dr. Johnson's phrase). We see the novelist behind the reviewer in comments such as :'although choosing to remain on the surface, she is an excellent diver' (of Jane Austen); 'though they (the plots) do not come out of the characters, yet they often give an impression of doing so' (of Helen Prothero Lewis); 'not only caring for the rudimentary meanings (of words), but for the finest gradations, the faint implications' (of André Maurois).

In discussing novelists, she reveals her own views on the art of the novel. We find a distillation, an underlining of some of those themes and ideas variously embodied in her novels which give coherence to her imaginative world. Writing, for instance, about the spirit of place in Grant Watson's Australian books, she emphasises what is the essence of her own, pointing out that 'it is the cumulative effect which counts in work of this kind.' And in 'Irony And Mrs. Wharton', she expresses her requirement that characters in country novels should 'move before the landscape as emanations of it.' Here and there she tends to didacticism (as in her novels)—for example, her impassioned definition of the true 'child of earth' (in the review 'Contrast'), which sprang directly from personal experience. Some interesting comments reveal her understanding of the creative process: she was keenly interested in psychology, 'the creative mind and especially the mind of the poet.' Reviewing 'The Art of Thought' by Graham Wallas, she praises his emphasis on the importance of the subconscious and intuition in the creation of imaginative literature—a theme to which she returns repeatedly in her reviews (*The Spectator* as well as *The Bookman*), and on which she expounds at length in the remarkable short essay, 'The Core of Poetry' (*The English Review*, 1919).

Introducing the third section ,'Poems', I must emphasize at once that the group of poems assembled here should not be regarded as representative of her work as a poet. This will be obvious immediately to those already familiar with her poetry. Gathered here are previously unpublished pieces and some earlier work including her earliest extant poems. In presenting these I consider their real value to lie not in any special merit as poetry, but in the evidence they yield of both her poetic and spiritual development. My intention is that this minor group will be complementary to the work of her mature achievement collected in my forthcoming volume *Mary Webb: Selected Poems*, in which I have brought together her finest poems to show her gifts to best advantage.

The juvenilia—poems written at Stanton-upon-Hine Heath and during her first years at Maesbrook, Meole Brace—are of more than biographical interest. Here the young poet Gladys Meredith is learning her craft, attentive to form, concentrating on perfecting rhyme and metre, and at the same time trying to impower her words with her intense feeling for nature.The earliest extant poem, 'Spring', dated 1898, may be taken as typical of many she was writing at this period, often imitative of her father's verse or of major poets she admired. Much of her early work she destroyed, dissatisfied with her attempts, knowing that she was still aspiring rather than achieving. Yet there is charm, sincerity, eagerness, poetic emotion in even the slightest of these poems—and precision of form.

Some of the Maesbrook pieces reveal her developing mysticism, her movement away from the conventional religion and orthodoxy of her upbringing. In poems such as 'The White Moth', 'I worship the earth . . .', 'The Gates Of Gold And Green', 'The Fawn', she expresses with youthful joy and optimism her ecstatic union with nature. For Mary, nature was church, refuge, source of renewal, and her spiritual relationship with it (specifically as experienced in the Shropshire countryside) is evident everywhere in her work, poetry and prose alike. This pantheistic mysticism is clearly the impulse behind many of her earlier poems (explicit in the incomplete 'calendar sequence').

ACKNOWLEDGEMENTS

I am grateful to the following for their kind permission to reprint the works of Mary Webb included in this book:

Hutchinson Publishing Group Ltd. for 'Mr. Tallent's Ghost' from *The Ghost Book*, ed. Lady Cynthia Asquith, 1926; 'The Cuckoo Clock' from *Sails of Gold*, ed. Lady Cynthia Asquith, 1927.

The Cornhill Magazine for 'The Sword'.

Country Life for 'A Cedar-Rose'.

The Caradoc and Severn Valley Field Club for 'Glimpses of Old Shropshire' from *Transactions*, Vols. VII and VIII, 1923.

The Spectator for reviews by Mary Webb, 1922-5.

Hodder & Stoughton Ltd. for reviews by Mary Webb in *The Bookman*, 1925-7.

Cassell & Co. Ltd. for articles by Mary Webb in *T.P.'s And Cassell's Weekly*, 1924-6.

Anthony Rota and Bertram Rota Ltd. for *The Chinese Lion*.

The Executors of the Mary Webb Estate, and Jonathan Cape Ltd.

My warm thanks are extended also to H. Bradley Martin for access to his private collection of Mary Webb's poems, and permission to publish these; to Raymond Lister, Honorary Senior Member of University College, Cambridge, for some invaluable references and for so generously giving me encouragement; and to Hilda L. Addison, the first biographer of Mary Webb, for her constant support.

I wish to express my appreciation of the help given by the Staff of the University of Liverpool Library, and particularly the University Inter-Library Loans Service; the Staff of the Local Studies Department, Shrewsbury Library, Shropshire County Library; and *The Spectator* Librarian, C. A. Seaton, for assistance in compiling details of Mary Webb's contributions to the journal.

G.M.C.

SHORT STORIES

A CEDAR-ROSE

WHEN you go down the lime-bordered path, jubilant with birds, to visit the Misses Amory, it is well to leave the vivid present at the garden gate, where you ring and wait like Christian for entrance. They are timid souls, and lock themselves into their fortress-like house in its enclosed garden, for fear of tramps.

Quite a little while after ringing, you hear the bell sound softly from a distance, as if it echoed down the dim passages of years.

Here the Past sleeps, still as the Sleeping Beauty, but of a relentless plainness of feature, for the youth of the Misses Amory held no romance. No gay lover ever stood in his stirrups for a glimpse into the garden, no clamorous manhood ever pealed the bell.

'How safe you are in here, Betty!' I said once to the little handmaid as she let me in.

'Too safe by far, Miss,' she answered, wistfully, lingering near the gate with the look in her eyes of one who listens for a known step.

The path leads between privet hedges to the plain old house, which you enter through a glass porch all in a green haze of ferns.

No scent of dried rose leaves or lavender meets you on the threshold, for the garden never grew flowers, being too much overshadowed by an immense cedar, the pride of the old ladies' hearts. The plain rooms are permeated with the clean aroma of the spreading boughs, under which these lives came into the world, grew to womanhood, and have now grown old. Below the eastern windows is a little lawn, covered towards autumn with round, green cedar fruit.

'It is so terribly untidy, my dear,' Miss Jane always says with a sigh; 'but I cannot engage a boy to gather them up, for what would the birds do if a noisy boy came in here?'

It is truly an unanswerable problem, for the birds are the real owners of the house and garden; they build in the bedrooms, go to roost in the sacred cedar and have a safe home in the old ladies' hearts. The steep garden is a place of half-lights and grey rockwork, where still remain the little pools and disused fountains loved by childish imaginations, and high on the house still hangs the bell which used to call in three good little girls to bed.

Sometimes when the wind is moaning in the cedar it tolls the bell, and it is as though the spirit hands of their austere father still held the rope. There is no need now for a bedtime bell—they are quite ready for rest at the end of their busy day, and rheumatism waits to seize them in the damp garden at dusk.

Their occasional tea-parties, always limited to one guest—for they do not feel equal to entertaining more at a time—are held on the lawn only in the hottest weather, where it is restful and cool beneath the dark boughs.

One hot day we sat down to rest there after a busy and strenuous tidying of the little green fruit. We gathered it in baskets and took these down the mossy path and emptied them into the stream. How glad I should be to collect all the unnecessary little worries and cares of these two people and throw them far out into Lethe!

Miss Jane having gone in to make the tea (it was Betty's 'afternoon out') and having refused proffered help, Miss Adalia and I conversed about the usual topics, which hold an ever new delight when treated with her sweet and tender insight. We touched on the growth of 'our tree,' the callow brood at that moment being arranged by careful parents on a lower bough and the satisfactory improvement brought about by our afternoon's work. Then Miss Adalia looked up into the boughs and sighed.

'Ah! my dear,' she said, 'if it would but bear a cedar-rose!'

The very existence of such a delightful thing had been hitherto unknown to me, so I asked her to tell me about it.

'I never saw one myself, dear,' she said; 'but they are beautiful as they are rare. Once in a number of years one or two will appear on a cedar tree among the common fruit. They are rose-coloured, with curving petals, only in scent and substance unlike garden roses. They are like fir-cones to touch, and they have the fragrance of cedar-wood. I do not know by what law it is that they appear so seldom; Mary was our botanist, she would have told you.' (Mary's footsteps having wandered thirty years ago into the garden of Eternity, the question must wait.) 'Our tree has not borne one for more than seventy years,' continued Miss Adalia. 'Not since our mother found one when she came into the garden on her wedding day. That was before the railways, and father had brought her on a pillion from her home in Cheswardine. Well, my dear, whether it was its rarity, or our mother's finding it on such an auspicious occasion, or whether it was merely the wayward imagination of a child, I cannot say, but I always thought that the finding of a cedar-rose meant a happy life for the finder. Do not think me very foolish if I confess that the happiness I dreamt of was a little romantic. We were never allowed, and rightly, to read novels, but there are beautiful stories in the Bible, and it was of a joy like Rachel's that I sometimes dreamt. Not very often, for we were sensibly brought up, and I never spoke of it to anyone but Mary. Still, that was what the blossoming of a cedar-rose meant for me.'

So year by year had her gentle eyes looked for this blossom of joy and never found it. She had not wanted rose gardens or riotously scented parterres—only this one rather sombre flower, fit ornament of a sombre life. Such a little would have done! Some staid farmer whom she would have idolised and surrounded with comfort, and who would have given her quiet affection: she would not have desired the tropical splendours of love; and if her bliss were to be very perfect, a child to inhabit the warm house of her heart. Just one cedar-rose! Many less worthy have much more; and here was she with only the common hard fruit of little duties and cares.

'I have been very happy,' she continued, as though afraid she had complained; 'we had a happy life, Jane and Mary and I, while our mother lived; and even after her death—though we sadly missed her—our home was a united one and dear father ever kind, if not indulgent. He did not like society, so we saw few people and seldom went out; but Jane had her house-keeping and visiting of the poor, Mary her botany and I my painting; and then father was so clever, and would sometimes talk to us and teach us most interesting things.'

The pity of it! What were the gallants of the fifties doing, what was Mother Nature doing, that this should have happened? Because Miss Adalia was plain of feature, untalented in mind and secluded in life, there was no reason why she should not have fulfilled her woman's vocation. For she was not made to be a worker like Miss Jane; even her paintings are pathetically faulty in technique, her art is not great enough to shadow forth her fluttering yearnings. The earliest are the best, reminiscences of her gala days, when she and her sisters were driven by their father in 'the chaise' to some outlying farm, coming home along the winding country roads at dusk with a delightful sense of adventure accomplished. As I said good-night—Miss Jane having gone to fetch the gate key—Miss Adalia asked me gravely if I thought the blooming of a cedar flower before her death too small a thing to pray for. It was with the reiterated 'why?' which we all hurl at circumstance sometimes that I went under the limes, where the dusk was piercingly sweet with the drooping flowers, and the birds were fluffing their feathers softly for the night.

It must have been about ten days later that I stood at the gate, again with a bunch of roses in my hand, listening to the distant bell, the bees in the privet and the robins.

'Oh! Miss,' exclaimed Betty when she saw me, 'Miss Adalia she wur main bad one mornin', and she swounded right away, and I run to Jim, and

Jim 'e run like the wind for the doctor!'

Being much concerned about the first part of the sentence, it was not until afterwards that I enquired concerning the 'Jim' to whom Betty so naturally fled and who possessed such a Grecian accomplishment, and lit upon an idyll in the making.

Miss Adalia was on the little lawn, as the day was very hot, and welcomed me as usual with her reserved sweetness of courtesy. The freshness of the cedar, which is more an atmosphere than a scent, encompassed us, just as the old ladies' homely goodness breathes about them. Theirs is no incense-like saintliness nor the desperate sweetness of passionate self-sacrifice; it is just natural wholesome righteousness. Sitting so, beneath the sun-resisting boughs, with a tame robin singing shrilly and gladly above, and the distant tones of Miss Jane admonishing Betty, the one miracle of Miss Adalia's life was shown to me. Her face was young again as she slowly and mysteriously unfolded her hands, which had lain in her lap one upon the other; and there, glowing on her black dress like sunrise over yew trees, was what I knew at once to be a cedar-rose. How and whence had it come so unexpectedly? Looking up into the density of foliage, I wondered how those solid branches could bear anything so fragile-looking, so delicate, as this. Looking at her transfigured face, the wonder grew.

'Oh, my dear!' she said, in a breathless tone of rapture. 'On Friday morning early, when I came to feed the robins as usual, I was standing just here, and suddenly there came a little stir of wind above, and something fell softly—so softly—on the grass. And there at my feet was the cedar-rose!' Her voice quite shook with joy. 'Look at it, dear; you may never see another. See the delicate petals, the faint pink colour, the lovely shape. It must have budded and blossomed on some hidden branch high up, and that was why I never saw it.' Then she added softly, as if to herself: 'So long in coming, but so lovely when it came.' Then she turned enquiringly to me. 'What can it mean? I am sure it prophesies something wonderful for me. It is childish and superstitious, I know; but I cannot help regarding it as a herald of coming joy.'

'I hope so, dear Miss Adalia,' was all I could say, for what bloom of youth and its happiness could come now to this tired woman of seventy? What would ease, travel or riches do for her now? Away from her sheltered nook she would be unhappy; ease she did not desire; of money she had enough. Yet here she was, with eyes alight with longing, watching my face and waiting almost with awe for the naming of the coming joy.

'What can it be?' she wondered.

A hint of wind arose, for the air was electric with coming thunder, sending down showers of green balls on our tidied lawn, and, swaying the high old bell, drew from it the echo of a sound.

'Wait and see, Miss Adalia,' I said, with a laugh, though tears were nearer; and she laughed, too, and closed her hands upon her flower as Miss Jane came out to summon us to tea. Miss Jane was evidently worrying a good deal about her sister's 'indisposition,' to which the doctor had as yet given no name; but outwardly she was very bracing. Only after tea, when she went with me down to the stream at the foot of the garden, while we gazed down into the brown, still water, which always typifies Lethe to me, she asked anxiously if I saw any change in Miss Adalia.

'Sometimes she looks so like Mary did, and it makes me anxious, for Mary died of a decline, you know.'

She was much relieved at my assurance that no change was apparent to me, and said that she hoped great things from the doctor's next visit, as it was now nearly a week since he last saw her sister on Friday, the day she fainted in the garden. When Miss Adalia said good-night to me, she told me that she meant to 'confide in Jane about the rose,' as she thought it only right. I wondered what that lady of sound practical sense would say to her sister's day-dreams.

My one idea was to devise some pleasure which should fitly fulfil the flower's prophecy. But the unaccustomed is not sweet to age, peace is better than intenser joys, and there seemed nothing to be done. However, one day I met the doctor by chance and, asking his advice on the subject, found that things were arranged without my feeble intervention. My schemes were un-necessary, even as my sorrow was useless. In a

very little while now a wind will stir the shadowy
depths of the cedar, swaying the bedtime bell
into whispering vibrations, and drawing away
Miss Adalia's spirit out of the silent house and
garden over the river of Lethe. Then, at last, her
life's dark cedar will bear its immortal flower.

MR. TALLENT'S GHOST

THE first time I ever met Mr. Tallent was in the late summer of 1906, in a small, lonely inn on the top of a mountain. For natives, rainy days in these places are not very different from other days, since work fills them all, wet or fine. But for the tourist, rainy days are boring. I had been bored for nearly a week, and was thinking of returning to London, when Mr. Tallent came. And because I could not 'place' Mr. Tallent, nor elucidate him to my satisfaction, he intrigued me. For a barrister should be able to sum up men in a few minutes.

I did not see Mr. Tallent arrive, nor did I observe him entering the room. I looked up, and he was there, in the small firelit parlour with its Bible, wool mats and copper preserving pan. He was reading a manuscript, slightly moving his lips as he read. He was a gentle, moth-like man, very lean and about six foot three or more. He had neutral coloured hair and eyes, a nondescript suit, limp-looking hands and slightly turned-up toes. The most noticeable thing about him was an expression of passive and enduring obstinacy.

I wished him good evening, and asked if he had a paper, as he seemed to have come from civilisation.

'No,' he said softly, 'no. Only a little manuscript of my own.'

Now, as a rule I am as wary of manuscripts as a hare is of greyhounds. Having once been a critic, I am always liable to receive parcels of these for advice. So I might have saved myself and a dozen or so of other people from what turned out to be a terrible, an appalling, incubus. But the day had been so dull, and having exhausted Old Moore and sampled the Imprecatory Psalms, I had nothing else to read. So I said, 'Your own?'

'Even so,' replied Mr. Tallent modestly.

'May I have the privilege?' I queried, knowing he intended me to have it.

'How kind!' he exclaimed. 'A stranger, knowing nothing of my hopes and aims, yet willing to undertake so onerous a task.'

'Not at all!' I replied, with a nervous chuckle.

'I think,' he murmured, drawing near and, as it were, taking possession of me, looming above me with his great height, 'it might be best for me to read it to you. I am considered to have rather a fine reading voice.'

I said I should be delighted, reflecting that supper could not very well be later than nine. I knew I should not like the reading.

He stood before the cloth-draped mantelpiece.

'This,' he said, 'shall be my rostrum.' Then he read.

I wish I could describe to you that slow, expressionless, unstoppable voice. It was a voice for which at the time I could find no comparison. Now I know that it was like the voice of the loud speaker in a dull subject. At first one listened, taking in even the sense of the words. I took in all the first six chapters, which were unbelievably dull. I got all the scenery, characters, undramatic events clearly marshalled. I imagined that something would, in time, happen. I thought the characters were going to develop, do fearful things or great and holy deeds. But they did nothing. Nothing happened. The book was flat, formless, yet not vital enough to be inchoate. It was just a meandering expression of a negative personality, with a plethora of muted, borrowed, stale ideas. He always said what one expected him to say. One knew what all his people would do. One waited for the culminating platitude as for an expected twinge of toothache. I thought he would pause after a time, for even the most arrogant usually do that, apologising and at the same time obviously waiting for one to say, 'Do go on, please.'

This was not necessary in his case. In fact, it was impossible. The slow, monotonous voice went on without a pause, with the terrible tirelessness of a gramophone. I longed for him to whisper or shout—anything to relieve the tedium. I tried to think of other things, but he read too distinctly for that. I could neither listen to him nor ignore him. I have never spent such an evening. As luck would have it the little maidservant did not achieve our meal till nearly ten o'clock. The hours dragged on.

At last I said: 'Could we have a pause, just for a few minutes?'

'Why?' he enquired.

'For . . . for discussion,' I weakly murmured.

'Not,' he replied, 'at the most exciting moment. Don't you realise that now, at last, I have worked up my plot to the most dramatic moment? All the characters are waiting, attent, for the culminating tragedy.'

He went on reading. I went on awaiting the culminating tragedy. But there was no tragedy. My head ached abominably. The voice flowed on, over my senses, the room, the world. I felt as if it would wash me away into eternity. I found myself thinking, quite solemnly:

'If she doesn't bring supper soon, I shall kill him.'

I thought it in the instinctive way in which one thinks it of an earwig or a midge. I took refuge in the consideration, how to do it? This was absorbing. It enabled me to detach myself completely from the sense of what he read. I considered all the ways open to me. Strangling. The bread knife on the sideboard. Hanging. I gloated over them. I was beginning to be almost happy, when suddenly the reading stopped.

'She is bringing supper,' he said. 'Now we can have a little discussion. Afterwards I will finish the manuscript.'

He did. And after that, he told me all about his will. He said he was leaving all his money for the posthumous publication of his manuscripts. He also said that he would like me to draw this up

for him, and to be trustee of the manuscripts.

I said I was too busy. He replied that I could draw up the will to-morrow.

'I'm going to-morrow,' I interpolated passionately.

'You cannot go until the carrier goes in the afternoon,' he triumphed. 'Meanwhile, you can draw up the will. After that you need do no more. You can pay a critic to read the manuscripts. You can pay a publisher to publish them. And I in them shall be remembered.'

He added that if I still had doubts as to their literary worth, he would read me another.

I gave in. Would anyone else have done differently? I drew up the will, left an address where he could send his stuff, and left the inn.

'Thank God!' I breathed devoutly, as the turn of the lane hid him from view. He was standing on the doorstep, beginning to read what he called a pastoral to a big cattle-dealer who had called for a pint of bitter. I smiled to think how much more he would get than he had bargained for.

After that, I forgot Mr. Tallent. I heard nothing more of him for some years. Occasionally I glanced down the lists of books to see if anybody else had relieved me of my task by publishing Mr. Tallent. But nobody had.

It was about ten years later, when I was in hospital with a 'Blighty' wound, that I met Mr. Tallent again. I was convalescent, sitting in the sun with some other chaps, when the door opened softly, and Mr. Tallent stole in. He read to us for two hours. He remembered me, and had a good deal to say about coincidence. When he had gone, I said to the nurse, 'If you let that fellow in again while I'm here, I'll kill him.'

She laughed a good deal, but the other chaps all agreed with me, and as a matter of fact, he never did come again.

Not long after this I saw the notice of his death in the paper.

'Poor chap!' I thought, 'he's been reading too much. Somebody's patience has given out. Well, he won't ever be able to read to me again.'

Then I remembered the manuscripts, realising that, if he had been as good as his word, my troubles had only just begun.

And it was so.

First came the usual kind of letter from a solicitor in the town where he had lived. Next I had a call from the said solicitor's clerk, who brought a large tin box.

'The relations,' he said, 'of the deceased are extremely angry. Nothing has been left to them. They say that the manuscripts are worthless, and that the living have rights.'

I asked how they knew that the manuscripts were worthless.

'It appears, sir, that Mr. Tallent has, from time to time, read these aloud——'

I managed to conceal a grin.

'And they claim, sir, to share equally with the —er—manuscripts. They threaten to take proceedings, and have been getting legal opinions as to the advisability of demanding an investigation of the material you have.'

I looked at the box. There was an air of Joanna Southcott about it.

I asked if it were full.

'Quite, sir. Typed MSS. Very neatly done.'

He produced the key, a copy of the will, and a sealed letter.

I took the box home with me that evening. Fortified by dinner, a cigar and a glass of port, I considered it. There is an extraordinary air of fatality about a box. For bane or for blessing, it has a perpetual fascination for mankind. A wizard's coffer, a casket of jewels, the alabaster box of precious nard, a chest of bridal linen, a stone sarcophagus—what a strange mystery is about them all! So when I opened Mr. Tallent's box, I felt like somebody letting loose a genii. And indeed I was. I had already perused the will and the letter, and discovered that the fortune was moderately large. The letter merely repeated what Mr. Tallent had told me. I glanced at some of the manuscripts. Immediately the room seemed full of Mr. Tallent's presence and his voice. I looked towards the now dusky corners of the room as if he might be looming there. As I ran through more of the papers, I realised that what Mr. Tallent had chosen to read to me had been the best of them. I looked up Johnson's telephone number and asked him to come round. He is the kind of chap who never makes any money. He is a free lance journalist with a

conscience. I knew he would be glad of the job.

He came round at once. He eyed the manuscripts with rapture. For at heart he is a critic, and has the eternal hope of unearthing a masterpiece.

'You had better take a dozen at a time, and keep a record,' I said. 'Verdict at the end.'

'Will it depend on me whether they are published?'

'*Which* are published,' I said. 'Some will have to be. The will says so.'

'But if I found them all worthless, the poor beggars would get more of the cash? Damnable to be without cash.'

'I shall have to look into that. I am not sure if it is legally possible. What, for instance, is the standard?'

'*I* shall create the standard,' said Johnson rather haughtily. 'Of course, if I find a masterpiece——'

'If you find a masterpiece, my dear chap,' I said, 'I'll give you a hundred pounds.'

He asked if I had thought of a publisher. I said I had decided on Jukes, since no book, however bad, could make his reputation worse than it was, and the money might save his credit.

'Is that quite fair to poor Tallent?' he asked. Mr. Tallent had already got hold of him.

'If,' I said as a parting benediction, 'you wish you had never gone into it (as, when you have put your hand to the plough, you will), remember that at least they were never read aloud to you, and be thankful.'

Nothing occurred for a week. Then letters began to come from Mr. Tallent's relations. They were a prolific family. They were all very poor, very angry and intensely uninterested in literature. They wrote from all kinds of view-points, in all kinds of styles. They were, however, all alike in two things—the complete absence of literary excellence and legal exactitude.

It took an increasing time daily to read and answer these. If I gave them any hope, I at once felt Mr. Tallent's hovering presence, mute, anxious, hurt. If I gave no hope, I got a solicitor's letter by return of post. Nobody but myself seemed to feel the pathos of Mr. Tallent's ambitions and dreams. I was notified that proceedings were going to be taken by firms all over England. Money was being recklessly spent to rob Mr. Tallent of his immortality, but it appeared, later, that Mr. Tallent could take care of himself.

When Johnson came for more of the contents of the box, he said that there was no sign of a masterpiece yet, and that they were as bad as they well could be.

'A pathetic chap, Tallent,' he said.

'Don't for God's sake, my dear chap, let him get at you,' I implored him. 'Don't give way. He'll haunt you, as he's haunting me, with that abominable pathos of his. I think of him and his box continually just as one does of a life and death plea. If I sit by my own fireside, I can hear him reading. When I am just going to sleep, I dream that he is looming over me like an immense, wan moth. If I forget him for a little while, a letter comes from one of his unutterable relations and recalls me. Be wary of Tallent.'

Needless to tell you that he did not take my advice. By the time he had finished the box, he was as much under Tallent's thumb as I was. Bitterly disappointed that there was no masterpiece, he was still loyal to the writer, yet he was emotionally harrowed by the pitiful letters that the relations were now sending to all the papers.

'I dreamed,' he said to me one day (Johnson always says dreamed,' because he is a critic and considers it the elegant form of expression), 'I dreamed that poor Tallent appeared to me in the watches of the night and told me exactly how each of his things came to him. He said they came like "Kubla Khan."'

I said it must have taken all night.

'It did,' he replied. 'And it has made me dislike a masterpiece.'

I asked him if he intended to be present at the general meeting.

'Meeting?'

'Yes. Things have got to such a pitch that we have had to call one. There will be about a hundred people. I shall have to entertain them to a meal afterwards. I can't very well charge it up to the account of the deceased.'

'Gosh! It'll cost a pretty penny.'

'It will. But perhaps we shall settle something.

I shall be thankful.'

'You're not looking well, old chap,' he said. 'Worn, you seem.'

'I am,' I said. 'Tallent is ever with me. Will you come?'

'Rather. But I don't know what to say.'

'The truth, the whole truth——'

'But it's so awful to think of that poor soul spending his whole life on those damned . . . and then that they should never see the light of day.'

'Worse that they should. Much worse.'

'My dear chap, what a confounded position!'

'If I had foreseen *how* confounded,' I said, 'I'd have strangled the fellow on the top of that mountain. I have had to get two clerks to deal with the correspondence. I get no rest. All night I dream of Tallent. And now I hear that a consumptive relation of his has died of disappointment at not getting any of the money, and his wife has written me a wild letter threatening to accuse me of manslaughter. Of course that's all stuff, but it shows what a hysterical state everybody's in. I feel pretty well done for.'

'You'd feel worse if you'd read the boxful.'

I agreed.

We had a stormy meeting. It was obvious that the people did need the money. They were the sort of struggling, under-vitalised folk who always do need it. Children were waiting for a chance in life, old people were waiting to be saved from death a little longer, middle-aged people were waiting to set themselves up in business or buy snug little houses. And there was Tallent, out of it all, in a spiritual existence, not needing beef and bread any more, deliberately keeping it from them.

As I thought this, I distinctly saw Tallent pass the window of the room I had hired for the occasion. I stood up; I pointed; I cried out to them to follow him. The very man himself.

Johnson came to me.

'Steady, old man,' he said. 'You're overstrained.'

'But I did see him,' I said. 'The very man. The cause of all the mischief. If I could only get my hands on him!'

A medical man who had married one of Tallent's sisters said that these hallucinations were very common, and that I was evidently not a fit person to have charge of the money. This brought me a ray of hope, till that ass Johnson contradicted him, saying foolish things about my career. And a diversion was caused by a tremulous old lady calling out, 'The Church! The Church! Consult the Church! There's something in the Bible about it, only I can't call it to mind at the moment. Has anybody got a Bible?'

A clerical nephew produced a pocket New Testament, and it transpired that what she had meant was, 'Take ten talents.'

'If I could take one, madam,' I said, 'it would be enough.'

'It speaks of that too,' she replied triumphantly. 'Listen! "If any man have one talent . . ." Oh, there's everything in the Bible!'

'Let us,' remarked one of the thirteen solicitors, 'get to business. Whether it's in the Bible or not, whether Mr. Tallent went past the window or not, the legality or illegality of what we propose is not affected. Facts are facts. The deceased is dead. *You've* got the money. *We* want it.'

'I devoutly wish you'd got it,' I said, 'and that Tallent was haunting you instead of me.'

The meeting lasted four hours. The wildest ideas were put forward. One or two sporting cousins of the deceased suggested a decision by games—representatives of the would-be beneficiaries and representatives of the manuscript. They were unable to see that this could not affect the legal aspect. Johnson was asked for his opinion. He said that from a critic's point of view the MSS. were balderdash. Everybody looked kindly upon him. But just as he was sunning himself in this atmosphere, and trying to forget Tallent, an immense lady, like Boadicea, advanced upon him, towering over him in a hostile manner.

'I haven't read the books, and I'm not going to,' she said, 'but I take exception to that word balderdash, sir, and I consider it libellous. Let me tell you, I brought Mr. Tallent into the world!' I looked at her with awesome wonder. She had brought that portent into the world! But how . . . whom had she persuaded? . . . I pulled myself up. And as I turned away from the contemplation of Boadicea, I saw Tallent pass the window again.

I rushed forward and tried to push up the sash. But the place was built for meetings, not for humanity, and it would not open. I seized the poker, intending to smash the glass. I suppose I must have looked rather mad, and as everybody else had been too intent on business to look out of the window, nobody believed that I had seen anything.

'You might just go round to the nearest chemist's and get some bromide,' said the doctor to Johnson. 'He's over-wrought.'

Johnson, who was thankful to escape Boadicea, went with alacrity.

The meeting was, however, over at last. A resolution was passed that we should try to arrange things out of court. We were to take the opinions of six eminent lawyers—judges preferably. We were also to submit what Johnson thought the best story to a distinguished critic. According to what they said we were to divide the money up or leave things as they were.

I felt very much discouraged as I walked home. All these opinions would entail much work and expense. There seemed no end to it.

'Damn the man!' I muttered, as I turned the corner into the square in which I live. And there, just the width of the square away from me, was the man himself. I could almost have wept. What had I done that the gods should play with me thus?

I hurried forward, but he was walking fast, and in a moment he turned down a side-street. When I got to the corner, the street was empty. After this, hardly a day passed without my seeing Tallent. It made me horribly jumpy and nervous, and the fear of madness began to prey on my mind. Meanwhile, the business went on. It was finally decided that half of the money should be divided among the relations. Now I thought there would be peace, and for a time there was—comparatively.

But it was only about a month from this date that I heard from one of the solicitors to say that a strange and disquieting thing had happened—two of the beneficiaries were haunted by Mr. Tallent to such an extent that their reason was in danger. I wrote to ask what form the haunting took. He said they continually heard Mr. Tallent reading aloud from his works. Wherever they were in the house, they still heard him. I wondered if he would begin reading to me soon. So far it had only been visions. If he began to read . . .

In a few months I heard that both the relations who were haunted had been taken to an asylum. While they were in the asylum they heard nothing. But, some time after, on being certified as cured and released, they heard the reading again, and had to go back. Gradually the same thing happened to others, but only to one or two at a time.

During the long winter, two years after his death, it began to happen to me.

I immediately went to a specialist, who said there was acute nervous prostration, and recommended a 'home.' But I refused. I would fight Tallent to the last. Six of the beneficiaries were now in 'homes,' and every penny of the money they had had was used up.

I considered things. 'Bell, book and candle' seemed to be what was required. But how, when, where to find him? I consulted a spiritualist, a priest and a woman who has more intuitive perception than anyone I know. From their advice I made my plans. But it was Lesbia who saved me.

'Get a man who can run to go about with you,' she said. 'The moment *He* appears, let your companion rush round by a side-street and cut him off.'

'But how will that——?'

'Never mind. I know what I think.'

She gave me a wise little smile.

I did what she advised, but it was not till my patience was nearly exhausted that I saw Tallent again. The reading went on, but only in the evenings when I was alone, and at night. I asked people in evening after evening. But when I got into bed, it began.

Johnson suggested that I should get married.

'What?' I said, 'offer a woman a ruined nervous system, a threatened home, and a possible end in an asylum?'

'There's one woman who would jump at it. I love my love with an L.'

'Don't be an ass,' I said. I felt in no mood for jokes. All I wanted was to get things cleared up.

About three years after Tallent's death, my companion and I, going out rather earlier than usual, saw him hastening down a long road which had no side-streets leading out of it. As luck would have it, an empty taxi passed us. I shouted. We got in. Just in front of Tallent's ghost we stopped, leapt out, and flung ourselves upon him.

'My God!' I cried. 'He's *solid*.'

He was perfectly solid, and not a little alarmed.

We put him into the taxi and took him to my house.

'*Now*, Tallent!' I said, 'you will answer for what you have done.'

He looked scared, but dreamy.

'Why aren't you dead?' was my next question.

He seemed hurt.

'I never died,' he replied softly.

'It was in the papers.'

'I put it in. I was in America. It was quite easy.'

'And that continual haunting of me, and the wicked driving of your unfortunate relations into asylums?' I was working myself into a rage. 'Do you know how many of them are there now?'

'Yes. I know. Very interesting.'

'Interesting?'

'It was in a great cause,' he said. 'Possibly you didn't grasp that I was a progressive psycho-analyst, and that I did not take those novels of mine seriously. In fact, they were just part of the experiment.'

'In heaven's name, *what* experiment?'

'The plural would be better, really,' he said, 'for there were many experiments.'

'But what for, you damned old blackguard?' I shouted.

'For my *magnus opus*,' he said modestly.

'And what is your abominable *magnum opus*, you wicked old man?'

'It will be famous all over the world,' he said complacently. 'All this has given me exceptional opportunities. It was so easy to get into my relations' houses and experiment with them. It was regrettable, though, that I could not follow them to the asylum.'

This evidently worried him far more than the trouble he had caused.

'So it was *you* reading, every time?'

'Every time.'

'And it was you who went past the window of that horrible room when we discussed your will?'

'Yes. A most gratifying spectacle!'

'And now, you old scoundrel, before I decide what to do with you,' I said, 'what is the *magnum opus?*'

'It is a treatise,' he said, with the pleased expression that made me so wild. 'A treatise that will eclipse all former work in that field, and its title is—"An Exhaustive Enquiry, with numerous Experiments, into the Power of Human Endurance." '

THE CUCKOO CLOCK

THE dreadful fate of Sam Sinnable came about in this way. First, his uncle went to a bazaar and won an egg-cabinet in a raffle. It was a beautiful cabinet. It had little drawers and big drawers, with divisions in them all, and each drawer and division was labelled with a nice, shiny, printed label, with the name of a bird on it. The people who made the cabinet seemed to think Sam would stroll out before breakfast and rob the nests of the rarest birds, and they provided a large compartment for the eggs of eagles—Sea, Spotted, and Golden.

The cabinet was varnished very plentifully, so that it shone with sticky splendour and showed finger-marks beautifully. Sam and the younger ones, even Baby, could have their thumb and finger-prints taken in the proper way, like criminals, whenever Nurse was busy. Before Sam had had it for a week, it was so covered with interesting prints and with the pudgy marks of baby's fat palm, that it seemed quite a nice, friendly piece of furniture. But it was not. It was a Temptation. It had in it two blackbirds' eggs, and a sitting of thrushes'. Sam thought with despair that before the great day came when he should be able to open every drawer and find every division full of the right kind of eggs he would be an old, old man, like Rip van Winkle. And he noticed that grandfathers were not really keen about these things, though they pretended they were. It was always like the games people play to amuse the children. Sam hoped very much to get his egg-cabinet full long before his beard was white, and as his age was eleven and he had not yet begun to grow it, he felt that there was still time. All the same, he must miss no chances. This was when Sam began the Downward Career, going from Bad to Worse, tres-passing, playing truant, tearing his clothes, quite forgetting the golden rule his mother had taught him—One nest, one egg.

He took them all, even the tiny dozen of the Long-tailed Titmouse. Nests he could not reach he raked down, holding a basket to catch them. The duck pond, the dove-cote, the preserved pheasants in the wood—all these Sam robbed. The Golden Eagle's place was ingloriously filled with pigeons' eggs. But Sam's chief stand-by were the eggs of the commoner small birds, such as sparrows, thrushes, starlings and finches. He took so many of these that the garden and meadow were always full of the sound of the scolding and mourning of the parent birds. This was what, more than anything else, brought about Sam's ruin.

Now this is what befell.

On a summer night without any moon, black and muffled and still under the leaves, the Herons came for Sam. They came to his bedside and woke him—two tall policeman herons, in sad-coloured liveries of ash grey and black. They stood there, tall and silent, looking down at Sam as if he were a very small fish, and he felt as if the long sharp swords of their beaks were already run through him.

Then they spoke in hoarse voices, both together, very solemnly.

'Oyez! Oyez! Oyez! Sam Sinnable is summoned to appear at the Birds' Assizes, on a charge of robbery, wilful cruelty and destruction. You bin a scandal in Birdland, Sam, and therefore a Round Robin was sent, with a petition to the High Judge, the great Eagle of Snowdon, and he has called the birds to the Assizes, and you mun come along of us.'

Poor Sam thought the herons spoke very

funnily, like people in a long-age book. He supposed it was because birds are older than people, and can remember nothing later than Saxon. But he had no time to think of this. He was terrified by the way they eyed him—as if he were very tiny and a long way off, yet not too far for their swords to reach.

'So up you get, and away-to-go!' said the herons, speaking together, as usual.

It was terribly solemn, like the litany.

Sam got up and dressed, tears rolling down his cheeks. No sooner had he fastened his collar and tie, than the herons seized him. Spreading their great, soft, hollow wings, they plunged through the open window into the starless damp darkness.

They went through the leaves and through the leaves, over the leaves and under the leaves, and at last they came to the Birds' Assize Court.

As the herons put him down Sam took courage to whisper a question which he had been asking himself all the way. 'Shall you know the road back?' he asked anxiously. Back to bed and the kitten, and Nursery breakfast, with steaming porridge, and Nurse, cross but safe.

'There be *no* way back,' said the herons.

They stood at the entrance to the Assize Court, and in the pale light left from yesterday Sam could see enormous walls of trees standing about a round glade, carpeted with cuckoopint and birds'-foot trefoil. The trees were chestnuts and firs. Every chestnut was set with white, unlit candles of flowers, and every fir was set with white, unlit candles of shoots.

It was all very solemn and still, with all the leaves neat and close on all the other leaves, like feathers, and the candles without flames standing up in the yesterday light. Sam felt as he did when his uncle took him on the scenic railway. He felt sick. He also began to be very cross with his uncle. First taking him on the scenic railway and making him sick. Then giving him the egg-cabinet and getting him into this dreadful trouble. And yet he had had to be ever so grateful for both. And now here he was. Yes, here he was, in the soft, deep, mysterious night, standing in the enormous doorway of the Assize Court!

'There's nobody there!' he whispered. 'Please, Mister Herons, can't I go home?'

'There be everybody here,' they answered, 'A million bird-souls all told.'

'But I can't see anybody.'

'Folk may be here, there and everywhere, yet be not seen,' said the herons.

At this moment there began the strangest, most frightening sound. It was like the rumour in the trees before thunder. It was like the first low scattered groaning or cheering of a great crowd of people. It was like the grumbling and muttering of herds on the mountains, before they break pasture and go down to the sea. Only it was soft as the soft night, muffled as a funeral bell. From every part of the huge amphitheatre the birds spoke.

'Go back? Go back? You'll never go back,' cried the Grouse.

'See, see, see, see, see!' whispered the Grasshopper-Warbler, as if he wanted everybody to stare at Sam. The nightingale wept, the lapwing cried, 'Eh, me! Eh, me!'

'Wicked, wicked, wicked!' called the thrush, and the owls hooted, 'It's you, you, you!'

The wood-pigeons took up the cry.

'We *knew* it was you—we *knew* it was you!' they moaned, till the sound of their soft roaring was like the sound of the sea in a dream.

Swifts screamed high above the topmost outlines of the trees, in the no-coloured sky. Ducks quacked, coots clucked, wild geese gabbled somewhere in the shadows of the heavy roots. The woodpeckers, sitting all together on a long branch, laughed nervously in a conceited manner, for they were the telegraph operators, and had to tap out messages to be sent all over Birdland. Near them were six ravens, the reporters, who kept writing absent-mindedly on their shorthand books the words 'Never more.'

All the birds who scream, screamed. All the birds who croak, croaked. All the birds who scold, scolded. It was as if every leaf had found a tongue.

But suddenly across the tumult a voice clanged —a wild, mighty voice, harsh, yet with something golden in it. Looking at the place it came from, Sam could dimly see, throned on a blasted tree that shone sad and grey, the great eagle from Snowdon.

At the first sound of his voice every bird was mute.

'Let the Court of Assizes be pronounced open!' said the old eagle, and the place was immediately filled with the deep, rolling boom of the bitterns sounding their gongs. Six grebes, standing stiffly in their liveries of brown and white satin, stepped forward and announced in watery voices.

'Ancient eagle from Snowdon, my lords ladies and gentlemen, the Assize Court is now open!'

A long ray from the low hidden moon, which had only just risen, crept through the glade like a searchlight, streaming across from the ancient eagle to Sam, who stood with the great cliffs of trees on each side of him, seemed much too small for where he was.

The eagle lifted his head and looked full at Sam. His strong hooked face and his terrible blazing, golden eyes, made Sam feel swallowed up.

'Swear in the Jury,' said the Judge.

The Clerk, a grey-headed rook, with a worried expression, began fussing about. Sam looked to see where the twelve good men and true were, and saw them very comfortably seated on a big branch, embowered in the leaves of the chestnut. At least, eleven were seated. The twelfth, whose name was Mr. Titmuss, was hanging by his feet doing gymnastics. The clerk noticed him and said:

'Contempt of court, Mr. Titmuss.'

Mr. Titmuss came right side up, and explained that it had been the custom of his family from earliest times so to do, and that in no other position could he think.

'You ain't obliged to think, you silly fellow,' said the Little Owl, twisting his head round several times, like a screw-top pepper-pot, without disturbing a feather.

'Well, what be I to do, then?' asked Mr. Titmuss.

'Find out what his lordship wants you to say, and say it.' But Mr. Titmuss only said. 'Fie, fie, fie!' and swung to and fro with such energy that Mr. Willow, from Africa (one of the numerous Warbler family) was very much annoyed. He weighed so very little that it was as easy to shake him as to shake a leaf.

'By the sun, moon, and stars, what did they put this small fry on the Jury for?' asked the old eagle.

'The robberies, your lordship, were mostly in the homes of such,' replied the clerk.

At this a most tremendous twittering began. It was so loud that the frogs, singing sweetly in the swamp, were quite alarmed and sang no more all night.

'Silence in the court!' commanded the Judge, and the twitterings died out like candles on a Christmas tree.

'A strange thing it is,' said the eagle, 'that I should be fetched away from my cool eyrie, where from dawn to dusk I gaze upon the sun and ponder on Eternity, where nothing troubles, and no sound is but the sound of dew distilling drop by drop and slipping into the dewpond. And behold! here is only an assemblage of wrens, robins, and what-nots. Hasten, then, for at earliest dawn I keep tryst with the sun. Bring the prisoner into the dock.'

The herons led Sam to a hollow tree, ringed with dock leaves. They put Sam inside, and the court usher, a magpie in black, slashed with white, hopped forward with a bit of dock in his beak.

'The prisoner is in, my lord, and here is some of the dock,' he said. His idea always was to get a bit of a thing in his beak, and things *had* been said—but chiefly by human beings, who didn't count—about petty larceny in the matter of rings and brooches. But he was always so anxious to please that the birds hushed the thing up and hoped for the best.

'Are the plaintiffs all here?' asked the Judge. 'How many are there?'

'A thousand, counting the mothers, me lord, all here.'

'Divide by five hundred, reduce to decimals, strike an average—in short, do anything you like so long as you get them down to five. I won't hear more than five.'

So they did all those things to the plaintiffs, and there were left Mr. Twite, Mrs. Dipper, Mr. Butcher-Bird, Miss Linnet (she was Mrs. Linnet really, only being a professional musician it was thought to be the correct thing for her to keep on being Miss, although she was Mrs.) and Mr. Fern Owl.

'Are the witnesses here?'

'Yes, my lord. Everybody living hereabouts is a witness. Everybody saw him.'

'Us didna!' said the owls, who have a very countrified way of speaking, because they hang about the barns and stack yards in the evenings. 'Us was asleep. Baint witnesses. Us can go to sleep again.'

They all went to sleep immediately, snoring loudly, to show how annoyed they were at being hindered in their hunting.

'First plaintiff!' said the Eagle.

During the scuffling that ensued, Sam looked round in the bright moonlight, and was astonished to see, very high up on the tallest tree, a large cuckoo clock. Its round face shone with a dark lustre in the moonshine. Its long, white hands went creeping and creeping, like antennæ, which are insects' feelers, as if they were trying to get hold of poor Sam. Its fir-cone weights swung solemnly to and fro¦ across the moon, which hung just on one side of it like a second clock face. Sam wondered what it could be there for.

The Clerk of the court called out:

'Mr. Twite!'

The court usher fussily brought him in.

'I understand you accuse the prisoner of taking, with evil intent, your whole clutch of eggs,' said the Eagle.

'Quite,' said Mr. Twite.

'Five, I think?'

'Quite.'

'And you think he deserves the extreme penalty?'

'Quite.'

'My good sir,' said the Judge, 'you become monotonous.'

'He can't say anything else, my lord,' whispered the usher.

'Fetch somebody who can, then.'

'Miss Linnet!'

'Married woman?' asked the Eagle, frowning.

In a trilling voice she replied that she was.

'Why Miss, then?'

'A miss is as good as a mile,' murmured the little owl, waking for a moment.

Miss Linnet explained about being a singer.

'Silly,' said the Eagle, 'but now about the prisoner?'

Miss Linnet was looking very nice in a close-fitting brown hat and dress, with touches of cream.

She immediately trilled into song.

'Six eggs of palest blue
Within the hedge of yew,
Beneath blue sky,
Had I.
Where are they now, ah me?
There is the culprit. See, see, see!'

'Mrs. Linnet deposes that prisoner took six eggs out of her house with intent to defraud,' said the Judge, gruffly. 'Next.'

'Mr. Butcher-Bird.'

Mr. Butcher-Bird said that he had taken a nice house with an excellent larder, and had spent a deal of time and trouble stocking the larder with everything suitable to the children, who were just ready to enter the world when Sam came and took them. So now there was all that good food, and no family to eat it.

Mrs. Butcher-Bird at this point broke down completely, and had to be taken out of court.

'Mrs. Dipper!'

Mrs. Dipper was a stout, countrified lady, very tidy in her dark dress with a white front. She curtsied to the Judge, the Jury, the Clerk, the Usher, and the whole Court. In fact, she kept on curtseying all the time.

She said that she and her husband had built a commodious residence, with a pleasant outlook over the weir pool. They had four eggs in the house. They went out early one morning for their swim, and while they were away Sam came and scooped out all the eggs with his butterfly net.

'Thanks, my good woman,' said the Eagle. 'Next.'

Mrs. Dipper curtsied again, and withdrew.

The last plaintiff was Mr. Fern-Owl.

He said he and his wife believed in the simple life. They were camping in the wood. Late one evening he was helping his wife to churn, when he saw Sam take the eggs. Two, to be exact. And though he fled round and round Sam, and jarred as much as he could, it was of no use.

'Be there witnesses to all these sins?' asked the Judge.

A piercing silver roar of sound answered him. So many birds fluttered down into the open that they were piled up like autumn leaves.

'Gentlemen of the Jury, you have heard the evidence. Retire and consider your verdict.'

'Now sirs!' said the usher, resisting the temptation to put the little owl's quill pen into his pocket. 'Now sirs!'

He woke the little owl, got Mr. Titmuss right side up, and saw that Mr. Willow was not crushed by the larger birds.

'The Jury has retired, my Lord,' he said.

But in less than a minute they were all back again.

'Agreed?' asked the Judge.

'Agreed, my Lord. GUILTY!'

The cheering lasted for several minutes, and poor Sam in his tree began to cry.

'Then I pass the usual sentence,' said the Eagle, glad to get through so quickly, for soon now the sun would be climbing the eastern steeps of Snowdon.

'Sound the gongs of doom,' said the Eagle.

The sound of the bitterns' gongs went rolling gloomily out into the forest.

'Nuthatches, do your duty!'

Twenty nuthatches, swarming up, unloosed the pulley and let down the cuckoo clock, which was received by the grey geese.

'Prisoner,' said the Judge, 'you have greedily and cruelly robbed the homes of the birds. People who steal from others end by losing themselves. I condemn you to perpetual imprisonment, and as the cuckoo is the only bird who steals other birds' houses, a cuckoo clock is a suitable prison for a boy who steals eggs. Herons, do your duty!'

Sam had not a moment to think or to try to escape. The herons marched him forward, the magpie officiously held open the door of the clock, the herons pushed Sam in, and shut the door. And there, to this day, poor Sam remains. Dismally, as you pass some clockmaker's on a winter evening, you may hear him calling for help. Only nobody knows it is a call for help, because all that Sam can say is 'Cuckoo!' And nobody knows it is Sam, because he is dressed like a cuckoo. And the only breath of air he ever gets is when the little spring to which he is fastened with birdlime, darts forward at the hours and half hours for him to call the time. You may think how he must enjoy twelve o'clock!

So poor Sam never went home to nursery breakfast, and the kitten and Nurse. His mother called him in the flower garden, and Nurse called him in the kitchen garden. His brothers called him in the orchard, and his father called him in the wood. But all they ever had of Sam was his finger-print on the egg-cabinet. For poor Sam Sinnable was fast in the little square parlour of the cuckoo clock, and there he is to this day.

THE SWORD

RICHARD CLEDD was what is known among competitive mammas as a 'catch.' That no one had caught him was a mystery. When closely questioned as to their failure, girls would explain tearfully that, after one had gone a certain distance, and just as the intimacy promised to ripen into something else, one came to a glacier—or a volcano, they never knew which—in fact, one came to a standstill.

Golden heads nodded, like sleepy flowers, to his arm in the dance; lovely bare shoulders leant to pillow his dark beauty; flappers, daring as kittens, gave him butterfly kisses. He liked it. He laughed and gave them pretty things. He went to all the parties. But always, even in moments of wildest revelry, even with his greatest friends, his homeless eyes looked across the gaiety into the dark night beyond. Unsatisfied, he came to the houses of the great, the lovely and the gifted. Unsatisfied, he departed. There was a wistfulness in his eyes as he looked at people, especially at women. His friends said of him that he was the man who perpetually enquired for the goods that were not in the shop, not anywhere in the world. When the war broke out they said, 'This will cure him.' But it did not. He took his leaves as he took everything, quietly, rather sadly. He looked a little less often into the eyes of good women, and trafficked a little more eagerly with the 'daughters of joy' for their soulless comfort. He returned to the line punctually, cheerfully, competently. He was dependable, and men depended on him. When the world crumbled round them, and the crevasse of hell opened before them; when they were mown down as if by the fury of God, and left lying in torture, they would lift lost eyes to his deep, homeless ones, and feel saved. This was the more peculiar, as he had no religion to offer

them as a solace. He had no tenets or views. He was not ambitious. They gave him honours and decorations in a kind of despair of being able to get through to him and express their gratitude and admiration. His batman made a useful little bit of tobacco-money by holding exhibitions of these for the benefit of other batmen.

'There y'are now! There's our little lot. V.C., Cross, and the whole caboodle. Youngest colonel in the regiment. Eat me aunt if we ain't in for a Field-Marshal's outfit one fine day.'

Richard had the love of these men—a love not to be won easily. They could not explain it. One man said it was his voice. 'Stirs you up, it does, right down to your stummick.' Another thought it was his understanding way of looking at you. They could not express the sense of the deep, icy integrity which lay in his soul like a sheathed sword and made him as absolute, omnipotent, terrible and beautiful as a god.

He went his way, wistful, lonely. Not one of the flower-soft, bird-voiced, gazelle-eyed girls he met could call him home. They flung themselves at his feet. He politely helped them to arise. They offered all. He appeared not to notice it, and their all seemed nothing. They spread roses in his path, but beneath his chill, penetrating gaze the roses died. His expression was a challenge and a reproach to his hostesses. Their homage was courteously accepted, punctiliously returned. Their galaxies of beauty were danced with, dined, fêted. He went, it seemed, as far as he could. Then, with an almost audible sigh, he left them.

And at last, one winter day, in the most unlikely place in the world, he met her.

He was looking for a housekeeper. Being a bachelor, he went to a registry office himself, and the woman who ran the registry office was—she. He knew it the moment he looked at her. She was home. All the bloom and the blossom, the intolerable sweetness of the year, from the first chill snowdrop-bud to the final pomp of autumn, were here, now, at eleven o'clock of the forenoon, in the registry office.

He sat down, looking at her so long and so intensely that she was rather frightened.

'And what,' she enquired brightly, 'can I do for you?'

'Everything,' he replied, making no attempt to explain this curious statement. But in a little while after this admission, this breaking-up of a life's reserve, there came to him a sudden expressiveness. He talked to her as he had never talked to anyone. She was amazed, troubled.

'He has not dared,' she said to herself, 'to trust any human soul, for fear it should betray his trust.'

She sat very still, listening. Cries came from forlorn streets. Snowflakes fingered the window and collapsed into tears. The gas-fire gurgled in persistent commonplaceness. Across the table with its crowded files she saw his face—the face of Odysseus come up from the sea. She had no idea, would not have been influenced by the fact, that his was one of the greatest names in England, that he could talk with kings, buy duchesses. But she guessed that he would be too fastidious to wish to buy anybody. His face seemed vaguely familiar, as faces do when one has seen various renderings of them in picture papers. The black hair, touched with grey. The stern yet sweet lines at the corners of his mouth. The clean-cut eyelids, straight across the pupils as if to give an intenser focus. These she seemed to know. His very soul she knew also. She could feel the shock of it to the roots of her being.

It was marvellous that he, so obviously strong and self-sufficing, should have come to her out of that cold world of lost cries beyond the pane, like Blake's 'Little Boy Lost.' She, and she alone, could make him a 'Little Boy Found.'

She was afraid of this call to her greatest, most beautiful self. She wanted to lapse again into the registry-office lady, with her busyness, her trivialities, her little tea-equipage, little storms,

tiny victories.

She had been obliged to fight so hard for this rather dreary room that she had a fondness for it. She was contented as people are when they are living only with their second-best selves. She realised that this new self, once in command, would make life very difficult. There would be sacrifices, a giving-up of easy standards and slurred principles. Why had this happened to her? She wondered rebelliously while they sat there through the short, bleak day, with occasional intrusions from stout ladies of culinary capacity, breathlessly determined not to be 'put upon,' and tall young women with 'manner,' and mammas piloting prospective buttonses from whose lips the liquorice was not yet quite gone.

Through it all he sat there, with the same faint twinkle, the same slight, dry, wistful smile as he had worn many a time in doomed trenches, O.P.'s, and no-man's-land. He was bored, but the day would end some time, and they could go to a restaurant and talk; and was she not here? Had he not been looking for her ever since, as a small boy in a white suit, he had cried because the beautiful angel in the church window would not come down to him? He had found her now. Was he going to risk losing her for the sake of a few errant cooks?

At last the violets of dusk brimmed the streets. They were in a restaurant. They talked, with intervals of silence.

And again next day—many days. For he was not a hurriful man, though changeless in his few resolves, his fewer desires.

Life became for both a heaven sandwiched between generals who would wash and generals who would not.

In one of the immortal moments he learnt her Christian name—her strange, charmed, fragrant name, falling lingeringly on the air like cool petals.

'Eucharis.'

He was silent for a long while, savouring it, listening to the music of it.

'Eucharis!' The tall, white, unmatchable eucharis lily flowered in his heart. A holy, peaceful name, with a faint backwash of the chants of eucharistic feasts. Yet, as her name, stirring passion. She was so velvet-white herself, with that lucent, mayflower skin, those lips where sweetness and strength kept truce, that high, candid brow, the eyes with large pupils like a child's—wondering, as if just lifted from looking at a miracle.

He was melted, humbled, by her still grace. He thought he would have felt the same even if she had had no soul. But when her soul came like a gentle falcon to his hand, he could have shouted with laughter at the insane foolishness of other men. To have passed her by! Her, to whom all men must turn, in this seared, sin-scorched world, as those dying in the desert turn to a mirage of silver lagoons and large-leaved trees.

Many did turn to see these two go by. For he was known almost wherever England was known, and she had that air of otherwhereness, distrait as one newly arrived from worlds unseen—her silks and linens kept, it seemed, the lingering sweetness, her body was still fair with the attars, of Paradise. She had the air, which is a distinction in itself, of belonging to no time, country, sect or class. She had been exquisitely her own until through the arcaded forests of life he had glimpsed her, seen her spirit fleeing like light through the leaves, wavering, pausing, at last with his own intermingling.

When he had pondered on her name in deep contentment for a considerable time he asked her to marry him. They were in the registry office, but he had taken the precaution of bolting the door so that clamant ladies could not trouble them. Only the storm moaned at the house corners and snuffed at the threshold. Inside were daffodils, warmth and a steaming kettle, reassuring and homely.

'What I am so thankful for is that you are so utterly alone,' he said. 'I gather that you have no near relations. You have an air of detachment.'

She assented.

'And at our first meeting I thought—from your ring, your black dress, your manner—that you were a widow. And I could not help being relieved by it, because complications are so damnable. I seem to want the rest of my life to be absolutely smooth.'

'Yes.'

'Was he killed—out there?'

The room was still as the centre of a fiery wheel, as water under ice, as a forgotten grave.

A sparrow, starving and desperate, flung itself violently against the window and fell across it, dead.

The face of Eucharis seemed ravaged by some secret, withheld thought, some conflict veiled as a drama enacted behind many curtains of gauze.

'Was he killed, Eucharis?'

'He went out in 1914. On his first leave we met and on the next we were married. That very day he was recalled.'

Richard sighed. It was obvious that the sigh was not one of sympathy but of thankfulness.

'Was he killed?'

She crouched close to the gas-fire, her slim shoulders bent beneath an invisible load; her tall, slight body, which always seemed to him to make a gown look like a calyx, acquired, under the influence of something in her mind, a suave sinuosity.

'After this, dear, we will never speak of him again. It troubles you. But I must know whether he is dead.'

A bleak and dreadful discontent, almost a hatred of her, of his love, seemed to be waiting at the back of his mind, waiting to submerge ecstasy, and love, and the daffodils, if she should answer 'No.'

'Yes,' she said, 'he is dead.'

Richard was too much relieved to speak.

She started up, and stood swaying, so that he thought her like those Chinese plants that spring into leaf and blossom in a moment.

'You look,' she cried out in a strained, irritable voice, 'as if you thought I'd lied—as if you were trying to detect me!'

'Lie?' he echoed. 'You could not lie. Lie? Why, if you could lie——'

'What then?'

'Heaven and Earth would break up and God would fall plumb like that dead bird.'

'Should you kill me, if I lied? Should you take your beautiful shining sword out of the scabbard, and kill me?'

'Eucharis!'

'Your eyes would kill me.'

'Eucharis, you're overwrought. It has been too

much for you. We will never speak of him again.'

'Are you sure you would mind so much, if he were alive?'

'Mind? Why, my dear child, we could not be married. At least, not without endless unsavoury legalities, smut in newspapers. Why, Eucharis, here we are with a romance as perfect, as lovely as the *Vita Nuova*. I'd almost leave you rather than spoil it.'

'Never leave me, Richard!'

'No. Why should I? He is dead.'

She clung to him, and as a relief from their intensity he began to tell her rather apologetically of his possessions, his responsibilities, castles here and there, titles and sub-titles, privileges, obligations. She would be a great lady. She seemed almost terrified at the prospect. The wedding would be, of necessity, ceremonious. She must take her place in the world. And the poor little registry-office lady wept with such abandonment of grief that his words might have been her death-sentence.

But in time he reassured her.

'The past,' he said, 'exists no more. And in the future I shall be always near you.'

She said after him, as one telling over a list of treasures.

'The Past exists no more.'

And, after all, to a woman sensitive to everything beautiful, the new life came easily. Delicious colours, rare materials became, at a word from her, gowns like poems. She 'walked in beauty.' She became immediately part of the atmosphere, the central loveliness, of his life.

His relations were charmed with her, and one imaginative aunt invented for her a royal ancestry (in the female line and under the rose). He rushed her from place to place, restless until the final marriage arrangements were accomplished. His laugh was so ready, his whistle so gay, his face expressed such a deep fulfilment, that those who loved him were ecstatic. Old gentlemen, for whom romance had faded long ago, polished their spectacles and looked at the lovers over the top of them, chuckled, blew their noses, harked back to the seventies. Young men of confirmed bachelor ways glanced at the lovers and at once went out and bought a nosegay for Miss Somebody of

Somewhere. And the registry office, the war, wounds and dark weather, poverty, pain, cruelty, death and judgment had melted like tall clouds on a blue, sinless day of April.

It was early spring, four o'clock in the afternoon, and the day before he was to take her to himself for ever. Everything was ready. All the splendour and the ritual waited; their journey afterwards was planned to the uttermost golden hour. His house was full of spring flowers, and she, in a gown of pale gold, was the centre of radiance. She was, for the first time, dispensing tea in the fire-lit hall. She was dispensing it to him alone, and he took as well the blessing of lips and hands, for the delay had tried him. His love, which had waited half a lifetime, had something of the fierceness of starvation. The hall was rich with tapestries and old oak, tall clocks, armour, and a long, carved sword-cupboard over the mantelpiece. He was kneeling beside her, his arms about her, his head on her breast.

Suddenly, the bell rang. In the farther hall the butler's step could be heard.

Richard sat down, frowning.

'Why did you order tea here?' he asked. 'I would rather have had it where we could not be disturbed, beloved.'

'It was—the sword-cupboard,' she said. 'I wanted to remember——'

The butler was talking to someone.

An irritable, exasperated voice was arguing with him.

'I tell you, I *must* see her. Now. This minute. To-morrow? Oh, God! To-morrow won't save her. I've come to save her, I tell you! I've gone through—oh! I've gone through hell for her sake. I must see her—and the chap, Gledd.'

'Lord Gledd will not see you, young man,' said the butler, more grieved than angry. 'Nor yet the Marchioness of Gledd—as will be to-morrow—won't see you neither. And *all* the secretaries are that irritable I daren't go near them.'

'Secretaries? Fool! It's Gledd I've got to see. Here I come with a gift that's cost me——'

'A present, sir? Oh, I understand now, sir. It shall be listed with the rest, sir, and the secretary——'

But at this point the young man seemed to be going mad. A large, muscular hand shot out, and the butler violently retired. The young man walked in.

Richard stood on the hearthrug.

'Carry!' said the young man, 'I've come to give you your freedom. I've come to say everything shall be all right. But you must put off the wedding till the divorce is through, Gledd. Carry! Don't faint, my dear. Everything's as right as right. I knew something was up when you stopped writing to me in that infernal asylum. Nerve hospital! Not much! Then I saw your photos in the papers. Crikey, Carry, I *was* glad for you, though it hurt pretty well at first. I'd always hoped—— But that's nothing.'

There were tears in his eyes and his large, nervous hands were clenched.

'I always *said* you ought to be a great lady. And now you will! I *am* glad. I tell you it's a great day for me, this!'

He pulled out a hideous coloured handkerchief and wiped his eyes.

'I didn't know what to do for the best. I thought of keeping it dark. Then I thought only the straight thing was good enough for you, Carry. I tried to come sooner. But when I told that fool doctor my wife was going to marry a marquess, he smiled in the way that makes you see red, and ordered bromide. But I got away in the end. And here I am. And we can arrange it all, can't we, Gledd? It's only waiting a few weeks. Carry! Say I've done right! Say you're glad I've got free.'

His voice was hoarse, pleading.

Richard had not taken his eyes from him.

'You are her husband?' he said quietly.

The young man took a marriage certificate from his pocket-book and gave it to him.

'And you were invalided home? Not thought to be killed?'

There was a pressing, whelming eagerness in the question.

'Killed? No. Wished I was. I was shell-shocked. They thought I should never get better.'

'And your wife—didn't think you were killed?'

'Carry? Lord, no! Carry was a brick. She wrote to me every week in that damned hole. Sent me things too. I say, she's going to faint. Gledd!'

Eucharis was standing by the great oak chair on the opposite side of the hearth from Richard. Above the mantelshelf was the dark, carved sword-cupboard. Dusk had thickened, blotting the many-tinted spring flowers to one grey.

Richard lifted his intense, omniscient-seeming gaze from the wild, honest, tear-smudged face of the intruder. Very deliberately he turned towards Eucharis, swaying in her sheath-like gown, greyish now the light had gone, against the dark background of unshuttered night. And as his look settled upon her there was in it the same icy, fiery dreadfulness that had been in it once when he court-martialled a man for robbing the wounded. Steely, unpitying, his eyes forced hers to look at him. No word was spoken. Only the unchangeable judgment of his never-betrayed ideals consumed her as their looks met beneath the sword-cupboard.

Suddenly she snatched her hands to her heart.

'The sword!' she cried, in a strange, chanting voice. 'Oh! it is the sword!'

She fell like a snapped lily, and Richard left her where she fell, for he knew that she was dead.

Gladys Mary Coles
76

GLIMPSES OF OLD SHROPSHIRE

THE RETURN OF THE ROMANS:
A DREAM OF URICONIUM

IT IS a cold morning in early autumn, and the swallows are gathering for departure. We should hardly recognise the landscape for our own county, because, just as furniture makes a room what it is, so do fields and roads, villages and scattered woods, farms and open country make a landscape homely. There are no fields or farms, no villages, nor open country to be seen here. In all the plain between Shrewsbury and the hills, and over all the hilly country towards Bishop's Castle there is nothing but forest—dark, impenetrable, primeval. Beneath the Stiperstones, clothed in woods of oak and pine, is a small clearing, close to the village now called Snailbeach. This is the entrance to the Roman lead mine, one of the chief causes, it is said, for the Roman settlement in Shropshire, the mine out of which comes—so legend says—in the dusk of evening a Roman horseman who rides over the country with a ghostly lady in green.

Outside the mine, on this autumn morning, stands a young Centurion of the Thracian cohort, hawk nosed and dark of eye, waiting impatiently for the moment when the convoy will be ready to start. The light strikes on his steel helmet, breast-plate and greaves. He wraps his cloak about him, for the air comes coldly from the Hope Valley, and hardy as he is he cannot help feeling the change from Italy, whence he has recently come. His white tunic flutters in the wind, and he fingers his short sword absently. He wants to be gone. They are striking camp for the winter, and the low, solid-wheeled bullock carts are loaded ready for the journey. The Centurion hears the twittering of the swallows and wishes he could go South with them. For he does not share our love of Salopia. In common with all Romans he regards Briton as a lost land

of eternal storm, of ocean thunder, of everlasting mist and fog, of horrible crafty little blue-coloured men, who hide behind rocks and roll other rocks down upon the proud cohorts. To him Shropshire is 'the last place God made,' or as we say in the musical country phrase: 'A lost and forgotten place.' He sighs, thinking of the orange trees of Italy, the hot, blue days, the marvellous aromatic nights. Then he remembers that, after all, his boy is at Virocon, his dear and only son, and Placida, his faithful wife. And it is to Virocon that they are now returning. His face brightens, he gives a sharp order to his men. They are in marching kit—such a marching kit as would daunt the bravest modern soldier, surely. Not only a spade and an axe hang on their backs, and rations, and a tin basin to eat out of, but each carries stakes ready to drive into the ground at the appearance of an enemy, and each has a heavy spear.

The ranks form up, the drivers prod the bullocks with the butt end of their spears, and the convoy gets under way. Probably it went straight over the Stiperstones, where the old tracks are, down near the Gatten woods and over Cothercott or Longmynd, where traces of Roman roads, I believe, still exist. Probably, also, they went along the top of Lyth Hill. The road would have forests, chiefly of oak and pine, on either side of it, and densely tangled masses of willow, tinged to autumn gold, would cover the plain, where marshes lay, and large sheets of water, frequented by herons. Wild horses grazed in the clearings, the bittern's cry sounded wild and lonely, and herds of red deer crossed the Roman road on their way to drink at some pool long since dry. Hares, also, the soldiers would see, and wildcats, and sometimes a skulking wolf.

The day has grown hot before they reach Lyth Hill, and the woods are full of the sound of bees. If the convoy could still linger, stores of honey might be found in the trees. Sometimes the soldiers see a robin or some other small bird in the undergrowth, but such small fry find life difficult with so many birds of prey about—kites and buzzards, falcons and even eagles. Such birds as doves and cuckoos probably were not more plentiful than they are now, for though there was no one to shoot them, there were many more large birds to prey on them. Water birds there must have been in vast numbers.

At last the convoy stands on Lyth Hill and surveys the plain, where now we see in September golden corn, whence comes to us the sound of threshing. Nothing is there but a billowing ocean of forest. No sound comes up but the tapping of woodpeckers, the neighing of wild horses, the bellow of a wild bull.

The Centurion is working, not towards Shrewsbury, which did not exist at that time, but eastward towards the Wrekin, clothed in deep woods, and towards the only town in that lone countryside—the White City in the Woodland, the City at the Confluence of Rivers. It is, for the time, his home, his Mecca. He can see it very well, for the woods about it have been cleared, and its roofs of glittering spar catch the lovely western light of afternoon. He can see the twenty-foot wall and the fringe of wheat; the groves of young, edible chestnuts and mulberries, and the vineyards; the hazel spinneys and the gardens.

The men also are glad to see the town again. After a lonely summer the joys of town life, the comforts and revelries, the wives and sweethearts who are awaiting them so anxiously, are very pleasant to think of. Now they are in the plain once more, and before dusk they are marching along Watling Street, working a way to the river, and the graveyard, and the roads set with tomb-stones in the shape of pillars with portrait busts on them. They see the blue wood smoke stealing up into the evening air through holes in the roofs, they see the bright shops, the booths and the passing chariots. And as they watch, halting a moment at the gate, a boy rushes out to them, shouting in delighted glee, 'Father!' It is Deuccus,

the Centurion's little son, grown taller since the spring. But before he can give himself up to the delights of home the Centurion must report at headquarters. So he sends the boy back with the news to his mother, while he goes to find the scarlet-mantled general. The ox-carts lumber in and are unloaded. The men disband, going off to the oyster shops and the wine shops. At last the Centurion stands in his own doorway and calls 'Placida' and across the tesselated pavement comes his wife.

Supper is prepared. There are dishes of red ware piled with roast hare, venison and broiled trout. A pale blue glass bowl is full of mulberries, another of white grapes. There are drinking vessels of glass and there is wine in red flagons from Rome. The brazier burns warmly, sending out pleasant, shifting lights on the coloured tiles. And while at headquarters the General is writing with his iron pen the shipment order for the lead, and while the autumn wind rises and fingers the roof, the little family laughs and talks, dreaming of a return to Italy, away from the land of savages, where the ground is white-over for weeks at a time.

Alas! They were never to return. No wonder the Centurion hated Britain, since it was to rob him of wife and child. Their tombstone is in Shrewsbury now, and though the glory of Roman militarism is gone like thistledown, a fragrance yet lingers about the name of Placida.

SHREWSBURY'S ABBEY FAIR

IT IS a hot August day, with a mutter of thunder in the air. But the thunder is a long way off and nobody takes any notice of it, for Shrewsbury is in festal mood—just such a mood as one feels in the town on Flower Show day. It is the first of the three days of the great yearly Fair, the new idea of Roger de Montgomery; it is ordained by law, and blessed by religion, for the funds go to the Abbey Church. It is, in fact, 'the thing.' If you don't go to the great Fair you aren't anybody, you don't exist. And how nice, for once, that the thrilling thing should also be the ordained thing! So they all put on their best kirtles and jerkins and go off to the fair ground, which lies some where near the Gay Meadow. Shrewsbury is hardly recognisable. It is not so much a town as a collection of small holdings. Each house has its bit of land, its animals, its stacks garnered from the hasty harvest outside the walls. A great lake ripples near the Abbey, and the river is wide, shallow and reedy, fringed with willows. The original Abbey Church was very small and was of wood. But Odelirius, father of the historian Vitalis, determined to build a better one, and a monastery as well. In order to do so he enlisted the sympathy of Roger de Montgomery. 'Lo! On the river Meole, in the house you gave me, I will found it.' In those days if you asked a great Lord to contribute to any such scheme he neither looked glum, saying that times were bad, nor did he dip into his purse. He smiled and was affable, and dipped into the purses of the people he ruled. So Roger vowed a fund to the Abbey and placed his glove on the altar in great pomp, and proceeded to tax the burgesses very heavily. A girl had to pay ten shillings for a marriage licence, a widow paid a pound. If your house caught fire you did not get a nice insurance cheque. On the contrary, you paid two shillings to the neighbours on either side because your fire had probably burnt down their houses. And you paid forty shillings to Roger for no particular reason except that he said so. Roger endowed the monastery with twelve pounds a year, which, as someone mildly remarked, 'doth seem but a little.' He sent to Normandy for monks to act as architects. These monks were rather coldly received. 'Mean was their attire,' we are told, 'scanty their provision.' And no doubt Roger thought that if the keen Shropshire air made them hungry they would work all the quicker in their desire to return to France. They began, the history says, 'in the street called Foregate.' This site must have been a pleasant place then, as it is now. The great Wolstan preferred to stay here on his visits to the town, because it was so quiet. There must have been much birdsong there, for the woods came so close, and there was no sound of traffic, only the mass bell ringing musically and the sound of sandalled feet. It was Wolstan who prophesied that the Abbey would become 'the most glorious place in the town of Scrobbes-berrie.'

On this day of the Fair, the building was making good progress. Wood came into the town for it by the Eastern Gate. A plot of land where they might dig gravel had been assigned to the builders by Roger. Sandstone was lugged in heavy carts with solid wheels, probably from Eyton-on-Severn. And the stingy endowment had been augmented by the gift of a little wood near by and by the fishery rights in the Severn and the lake, and by various pieces of land belonging to Roger's underlords and barons. The river was low, so was Meole brook, and no doubt children paddled there, as they do still, their mouths

stained with early blackberries. In the hot sun-
shine the booths on the fair ground looked gay,
and so did the dresses of the richer inhabitants.
The illustrations to Chaucer help us to guess what
these were like, for fashions changed slowly then.
Only Chaucer's people wore the London modes,
and the inhabitants of Shrewsbury at that date
were, in point of time, further away from London
than the farthest Hebrides are now. Many of the
people at the fair were of the serf class, and were
content with earth-coloured garments. Dark-clad
monks passed amid the crowds; Abbots in
splendid robes from other monasteries in the
county; retainers of Montgomery; soldiers,
carters, brewers, vine dressers; men selling hawks,
or armour, or finery for the ladies; cooks, with
trays of venison pasties; jugglers, jesters, begging
friars, a nun or two; sellers of simples and charms;
waiters from the religious houses, and a great
many shock-headed youths of the type known as
'varlets' in romances. All these took part in the
Fair, paid their money, chose their fairings,
laughed and danced, ate and drank, and showed
their prowess at the games, while the dark-eyed
men from Normandy, with long over-robes
tucked into their belts, worked on at the huge,
elaborate plan of the building. Slowly there grew
up the refectories, the guest hall, with bedrooms
around it, the schoolroom and dormitories, cells
and storehouses, hospital, library, and farm
buildings, with the church as the centre of the
whole scheme.

THE CHINESE LION

WE WERE waiting, Marcus and I, with anxious dread, for the postman's step beyond the frosty window. And to wait for what one dreads, yet knows to be inevitable, is the hardest thing in the world—especially for young lovers, to whom the least incursion of the outer world is intolerable.

While we waited, I was embroidering, in faith and hope and a great deal of charity, the piece of silk which was to be framed as an overmantel for our future home. The design I had copied from a curious old plate which Marcus had brought back from one of his mysterious journeys in China. It was one of those bits of antique pottery which might, if not known to be of priceless worth, be thought mere imitations. The colour was a kind of dull grey, dimly glazed. On this were painted, in desultory fashion, curious leaves, flowers and branches. They were done in shades of red and blue—shades not known now, impossible to match in any embroidery silk. The nearest were light indigo and a kind of Venetian red: but in the plate the indigo had a tint of love-in-a-mist, and the Venetian red had something of the ardent colour of a red dahlia. And in the midst, enclosed in a naive ring of blue, was a strange beast which, if it resembled any known animal, resembled a lion.

Marcus said he had never seen a lion on a Chinese plate. I did not even know whether lions had ever lived in China. But we called it, for lack of a better name, the Chinese lion. It had a dour expression, but there was something so innocently childish in its technique that we felt an affection for it. Whenever he came, Marcus would say, 'Done the beast yet?'

But I had left the lion till the end, for, though his lines and curves looked simple, they were very hard to copy. They made me think of those emblems used for charms and symbols—such things as the Freemason emblems, the pierced hearts of Catholicism, the enclosed trefoil of the Trinity.

This morning, as we waited for the ringing footsteps we dreaded, I had finished the leaves and branches and the stiff, many-petalled flowers, and was beginning the lion.

Marcus, looking across to the window, said, 'There are some of your branches and leaves among the frost-flowers, Juliet. Your Chinese lion might suddenly appear there too if the frost held.'

And at that moment we heard the postman's footsteps ringing in the avenue. I heard them through the thick beating of my heart.

And he brought the dreaded letter. There would be no more happy week-ends, Marcus coming down in the car with Dad on Saturday afternoon; Mother arranging pleasant literature in his room—as if he could fix his mind on books, he used to say, when he was under our roof. There would be no more evenings when, in the pleasant firelight, Dad and Mother being mysteriously absent, my silks lay untouched and my thimble was enclosed, along with my ten fingers, in Marcus's large and capable hand.

For Marcus had got the job he had asked for —the dangerous (how dangerous he never told me) and difficult Secret Service job which would mean, if successful, glory and advancement and the swift materialization of the home we dreamt of: which would mean, if unsuccessful, death. It would take six months.

If all went well, he would be back in the autumn. In fact, he could not be back later than next Christmas, because the results of his mission would then be public property, and his only safety would be in immediate return.

And at once, in the heart-breaking way men have at such times, Marcus withdrew himself from my love and tenderness. He was suddenly hard, concentrated, impervious, apparently, to any emotion. I could not understand this. I did not realise that it was only a more far-sighted, more practical way of loving than mine. But Dad understood. When Marcus had gone, which he did at once, in a whirlwind of haste, Dad found me crying over this hardness in my lover. 'Child,' he said, 'if he hadn't put on armour against you, he'd never have gone. A chap ain't made of wood and stone, you know.'

Mother looked at him reproachfully from behind her large, swimming spectacles. 'John, my dear,' she said, 'in tragic moments you invariably say "ain't," and it makes things worse.'

They were both irritable with each other because they were so sorry for me. What made things so unbearable was that Marcus could not write to me. As soon as he left England, silence and invisibility would descend on him till the autumn. But then—ah, then! How the doors of ecstasy would open then!—Door after door swinging back to reveal the rose-coloured securities of the house of love.

When the dreadful feeling of utter vacancy, which his going brought, had a little passed over, I thought what I would do to make the time go —to force the heavy-footed days to rush past like frightened sheep. I would embroider not only the overmantel, but all the chairs and cushions for our sittingroom. They should be done in the same design, for there is nothing so soothing as slightly monotonous work. Dad called it my Penelope-stunt, and it certainly helped me to wait for my traveller. As I put in the small, close stitches in those strange colours which, for all their richness, were nothing to compare with the glowing beauty of the plate itself, I thought of Marcus out there, in those ancient Chinese mountains far away— blue mountains misted with legend, with in-numerable generations of men, with horror, and a savagery as curiously refined as the Chinese lion itself. There tamarisks floated in breathless pink along huge slopes, and massed snows toppled on pointed indigo peaks. I tried to put these colours, these strange dreams, into my work. But one thing I never could do. I never could quite catch the contours, the peculiar wise majesty, of the Chinese lion. Something escaped me, some touch of dignity, or brooding, or menace, in the strange beast. Was it menace? Or promise? It was impossible to tell.

Dad would look at me over his pince-nez, puzzled, sympathetic and interested. One day he said, 'I see six chair cushions in course of construction. Where are the chairs?'

'In the future, dear, with Marcus.'

'Well, well! We can manage the chairs. In the future, hey? Oh, they must come out o' that!'

'What's the matter, John?' asked Mother. 'What are you grumbling at?'

'All these chair cushions, and no chairs,' said Dad. 'Dam' well embroidered, too. Nice cushions like that must have chairs to show 'em off and people to sit in 'em.'

That very day he took me to an antique shop, and bought a set of the loveliest old knobby chairs, meant for embroidered cushions. After that, as each lion was finished, it was mounted, so that by the end of the summer a row of lions, each just missing the expression of the original, stood against the drawing-room wall. I had two months left in which to finish the one for Marcus's armchair. At any time now I might get my cable. For Marcus had said that when the work was done he should cable me the words 'Chinese Lion' as a joke.

There was reassurance, as the dark evenings drew on—evenings of autumn, that so strengthen homesickness, lovesickness—in working on the chair. For how could anyone, except a master of irony, believe that when the chair waited, glowing with love, there would be no one to occupy it?

But when the chair was finished, and the date fixed by Marcus was gone by; when morning after morning there was nothing, and evening by evening the obdurate silence was unbroken, then I saw that Dad was joining the believers in irony. He would go to the window and look out, and mutter, 'Bad weather! Dam' bad weather!' as if he meant to write to *The Times* about it. He did go up to town and put enquiries on foot through a friend in the Intelligence Department. But nobody knew anything of Marcus since June.

My chairs were done. They stood in a row, mutely demanding a home, all through the autumn days, that dragged their weary gold before my unseeing eyes. It was December. And if he had not cabled by Christmas . . .

'My dear! My dear!' cried Mother, 'It's coming for Christmas! Your cable's to be a Christmas card!'

But nothing came. On Christmas morning Dad stayed at the window so long that breakfast was cleared without his noticing it. And when he stared at the frosty garden and said in a hoarse voice—'Devilish!'—Mother, whose face was mottled with crying, said 'Devilish!' after him in a strangled tone, though as a rule no such word was allowed in her presence.

I was so tired. One day I thought I would stay in bed. After that, it was too much trouble to get up. Yet the faintest flicker of hope still remained to me. I set my mind on New Year's Day, for on that day, if all had gone well, we were to have been married.

If Marcus still lived, he would not leave me comfortless on New Year's Day.

The chairs, the overmantel, the cushions, were in my room now, and I looked at them in the dreary exhaustion of reaction, in the sickly-sweet fragrance of waxen winter flowers.

There was nothing to say, nothing to do, nothing to think. Yes! There **were** things to think! There were thoughts of Marcus to think— thoughts of anguished sweetness, and of such intense longing that they must draw him home. Pink tamarisk, and toppling snows. Blue and dark serrated mountains. Branches, leaves, and sweet, thick-petalled flowers. Pale china, grey, opaque. Pale silk. A naive ring of blue. The Chinese lion. Not a lion only, I was sure. No! An emblem, a talisman, a mascot. In ancient palaces golden lovers with long eyes and secret smiles had given it as a token. He, going, gloriously-caparisoned, to the wars, had it embroidered on his satin robes. She, when her babe was born, had it sewn upon the hangings of her splendid bed. Had she died—the golden mother? Had he, the golden lover, fallen in battle? Or had the lion, the cryptic,

the unrevealing, brought them safe again to one another's arms?

Two words, not long ones, and the world would be changed. Up the avenue, where the dark branches interlaced so sadly, there need only come a boy on a bicycle with a bit of paper.

'CHINESE LION.'

How foolish they would think it at the post office!

But when dusk closed in on New Year's Eve, there had been no cable, and a faintness came upon me with sleep, so that I hoped that I should die.

I slept with the heaviness of those that have nothing to wake for, and I dreamed of the winter day when we heard, beyond the frosty window, the feet of the messenger of sorrow.

I woke, and there was the frost again upon the window, heavily encrusting it with jungles of leafage, branches and fronds and strange flowers, all lit by the red, rising sun.

And in the midst of the window, curve for perfect curve, line for exact line—the Chinese lion.

You will not believe it, of course, though you probably profess to believe in the conquest of mind over matter, in telepathy, in miracles—so that they happened long enough ago. But there it was, and the deep red sparkles of the sun, the bluish colour of the ice, imitated strangely the colours of the plate.

I was out of bed, in Mother's room, sobbing, laughing, trying to tell her.

'It's come, mother! Oh, mother! The message has come.'

'What? On Sunday?'

Mother was always practical.

'No, no, mother!' I said, 'Not a cable. A Chinese lion!'

'Now, now, gently does it,' said Dad, coming in. 'Tell us, child!'

I told them.

'Go, John,' said Mother, 'and fetch Doctor Price this minute!'

But I made her come into my room when he had hurried away, and I fetched the maids, and they all saw it. It was there as plain as could be, as if it had been cut with a diamond. When the sun came out more strongly, it melted like an

enchantment. But it had been there. It had
brought its message. I believed in it so thoroughly
that the very next day I began to order my
trousseau.

Dad and Dr. Price were met by five awed
women who had seen a miracle. They were
obliged to believe Mother, for she is the most
prosaic person in the world. Dad looked at my
happy face.

'Weather ain't so devilish to-day,' he said.

Mother never corrected the 'ain't.'

And although the cable did not come for
another week, I knew Marcus was on his way.
The Chinese lion had saved my sanity and life
itself. And when it did come, it came from
Marseilles, and in no time at all Marcus followed
it. His work was done, and well done. But as soon
as he had reached the coast he had been struck
down with malaria. From hospital he had been
taken aboard the home-going ship, delirious. He
had been too ill to do anything or remember
anything till Marseilles. But in his strange dreams
he had thought of me, somewhere beyond a
frosted window, embroidering in rich soft colours
the sinister-benignant shape of the lion. He had
reached out to me. He had flung himself at the
frosty window to get through to me. He had
conjured the picture on the plate because it
brought him, he said, my face bent over my silks.

'But what I should like to know,' said Marcus,
'is this. Did your outgoing thought carve it on the
window, or my incoming thought?'

'You don't mean to say that you, a chap of
your intellect, believe in it?' said Dad.

'I do.'

'Besides, we all saw it,' said Mother.

'Pack of nonsense!' blustered Dad, for he was
terribly afraid of believing it. 'But it's devilish
good weather,' he added. 'If this ain't spring!'

And again Mother did not correct him.

ESSAYS, ARTICLES, REVIEWS

The cottage where she lived in Hampstead when writing the reviews.

Gladys Mary Coles

THE CORE OF POETRY

POETRY is the subconscious self breaking from its prison of silence and finding its way through the mazes of the written word. Very often it frees itself from the tyranny of the word, expressing itself, not through the thing said, nor even through the idea, but through a rhythm, a cadence, or a chiming of sounds.

No verse is poetry unless the subconscious self speaks through it. In its absence we get work like that of Pope and Browning—prose arranged in metrical form. On the other hand, all prose in which the subconscious is heard becomes, by virtue of it, poetry. So we get the echoing beauty of Synge and the Gospel of St. John. It is because there is so much of it in the works of Keats and Shelley that they are such amazing creatures, stalking through the mists of life like princes of Faery. They have not only the vital essence; they have also the chimes and the rhythms. But none of these outward things is indispensable; the miracle of poetry is beyond them, infinitely remote. Those rare utterances of the soul that remain for all time mysterious and thrilling—haunted words—are often of a childlike simplicity. That which peers from their little window and bursts from their narrow door knows nothing of mere architecture, and would be as little cabined by a temple as by a hut. Take such lines as—

'Listen! the mighty Being is awake.'
'Come unto Me, all ye that labour and are heavy laden, and I will give you rest.'
'The unimaginable touch of Time.'
'A solitary shadow wailing on the margin of nonentity.'
'After life's fitful fever he sleeps well.'

They are not merely beautiful; they are not only noble in idea: but they reverberate through time; they sound on into eternity; they have an affinity with something not of our world at all. Such things are great, not because of their context, for they shine out from it, whatever it is; nor because of their writer's aggregate of beautiful expression, for very often the poet of one slim book will suddenly startle us with a clangorous phrase like a great bell. It is just that, in the moment when the immortal line was written, the being that dwells far within the poet's deepest self was awakened by the stir of creative thought, quickened to some latent memory; so there sounded, startlingly, almost fearfully, in the midst of his music, a cry wild and unearthly—crude poetry. The unknown soul from whom once, in a single phrase, such poetry breaks forth is great, no matter how little he has written or (even worse) how much rubbish he has produced. James Clarence Mangan shines out because he said

'He too had tears for all souls in trouble
Here and in hell.'

So the school of Pope and Dryden become strutting pygmies, for all their immense attainments. By this standard almost the whole of contemporary poetry either shrivels or is revealed as prose—brilliant, but still prose. The few exceptions only make the waste more dreary by comparison. But these exceptions are precious. Although they do not thunder on us like the giants, they have the unmistakable cry. Walter de la Mare stands supreme among them, by virtue of such lines as:

'Sang down the faint reiterated call
Of those who came no more,'
'. . . the heart-dismaying shine
Of midnight streaming by.'

In these lines the subconscious, with low,

inward-sounding whisper, arrests us as mere music never could. It is also in the poetry of W. H. Davies, who knows the essence of growing things and the hearts of thrushes, and, with the spiritual hunger that only poets feel, eats of the leaves of the forest:

> 'No other noise but these green trees
> That sigh and cling to every breeze;
> And that deep, solemn, hollow sound
> Born of the grave, and made by Bees.'

What is this mysterious thing that inhabits the depths of man, glimmering there like an underwater town, sounding from the recesses of being like the plucked harpstring of a mermaid beneath the waves? It has an affinity with the intellect, but it is not the intellect—it is swifter and more unerring in its ways. It holds communion also with the emotions, but it is greater than they are —greater than the whole sum of them. It is akin also to the animal world, so that the poet of genius is more in tune with the bee than he is with the poet of talent. For the animal world seems to be guided along its dusky way simply by intuition. So the bee's cell of honey is an inspired poem, although it is a poem of matter. The genius works during his inspired moments in as blind a fervour of creation as the bee. In just such a mood Blake wrote:

> 'Calling the lapsèd soul,
> And weeping in the evening dew.'

If we could get at the subconscious self of the whole race we should reach a revelation such as there has never yet been. This can be done only through poetry. The more people express this self of theirs in some form of words, the nearer we get to it. It does not matter what the utterance is —moral or non-moral, egoistic or altruistic; nor does it matter how simple the manner of expression. The harpstring has sounded: a human soul has come forth to us, bringing out of the depths something strange, deific. Though words are only the wire along which the electric fluid comes, and though they might often have been better chosen, still it is doubtful whether any others, however beautiful, would have done the work as well as these which darted to the poet's mind with the idea. It is the vibration beneath the thing said that gives us the message and stirs us with awe,

just as the tremor in a voice often tells us much more than what is spoken.

> 'Good things of day begin to droop and
>   drowse——'

Has the homesickness for sweet, natural joys and wholesome days ever been expressed more perfectly than it is there? Yet how simple it is, and how little is said in mere words! Apart from the exquisite falling cadence of 'droop and drowse,' which is the inevitable artistry of great genius, it might have been said by any intense personality. Where then does the passion come from? We are forced to the conclusion that here the subconscious has asserted itself in such an unusual degree that it is almost independent of the words, running through the sentences as lightning runs through a forest. It was because Shakespeare had so great a share of subconsciousness that he was able to express the deepest instincts of the race and something that, lying beneath them, seems to be the nearest we have yet come to a revelation of God. It is through poetry that we shall come nearer to it. That is why the poet is a priest and the man who defiles poetry or touches it lightly is a blasphemer.

NEW YEAR CUSTOMS

'OLDE customs, that good be, let no man despise,' said Mr. Thomas Tusser, most didactic of agriculturists. There is truth in his axiom, for though we continually emerge from the past into better things, yet there are many ideas of humanity expressed in books or in folklore which are immortal, shining out like lamps beyond their dark century. And the greeting of New Year, of the springing blade, the sweetening air, life stirring in the tree and in the heart, is one of the best, as well as the most ancient of these.

In Shropshire there were, and I believe are still, many relics of fire-worship in the New Year customs. So a man who came each year to a farmhouse to bring in the luck said nothing, but went across the room and stirred the embers to a blaze. Some people employed a boy or a man to visit the house every New Year, paying him a trifle. His perquisite was a pint of mulled elderberry wine and a mince pie.

It was, and is, considered very unlucky for women to visit a house on New Year's Day. Possibly this mistrust of femininity is a relic of old monkish ideas. If a woman had a spite against anyone she would put on her best clothes, go to their house early in the day and pleasantly wish them a Happy New Year. After that there was 'no luck about the place' for twelve months. This kind of polite irony appeals as much to the half-Celtic mind of the Shropshire peasant as it does to the Irish. Fair-haired men were not in demand for this office of wishing good luck. Were they not descended from the lightning gods? By the same token a red-haired man would not do either.

No. He must be 'dark-favoured' as the winter woods, the tree-trunks, the furrows showing richly through the pale snow.

Mystery and silence are two of the salient features of New Year customs. One must 'greet the unseen' *not*, as a poet once fatuously said, 'with a cheer,' but in awed and humble silence. Every miracle of life waits beyond that threshold. There are snowdrops and the early palm, wedding bells, greetings on the highway of life, argosies of dreams, corn and wine in season, children making daisy chains with dimpled hands. So amid the sigh and whisper of the snow it is best to wait in quietness and trust for the day of roses. Only the companies of merry boys startle the winter morning darkness with their sudden song, clear as a missal-thrush's note:

God bless the master of this house
And the good missus, too,
And all the little children
That about the table go.

Gladys Mary Coles 76.

"Hark, how the Birds do Sing!"

Rapture of the Wild Orchestra in Full Melody

'A CHARM OF BIRDS' was a phrase used of old to describe the sweet noise of many birds singing together. It seems especially to recall the ringing, echoing sound of their music in the forest, of which Herbert says:

'Hark how the birds do sing and woods
   do ring!'

And Spenser:

'All the woods then answer, and their
   echoes ring.'

There is something in this charm that is not in any one bird's song—something at the same time wild and spiritual, the essence of birdland. To hear it in a June dawn is enough to bring tears to the eyes. It is fuller and sweeter then than at any other time, for every bird is in song, not only the home birds, but the early migrants and the late ones. Everybody answers 'here!' to that June roll-call. Nobody is thinking of departure yet. Even the cuckoo, though he stammers a little sometimes, is shouting with all his May vigour. The thrush, who sang in gleams between January snowstorms, is 'word-perfect' now, and his golden fluting has no harshness left in it. The wood pigeon in deep and tender notes is too melodious ever to be monotonous, and reminds one of Tennyson's delicious bit of word painting —'The moan of doves in immemorial elms,' where, in the long-drawn 'o' and the sleepy 'm' one hears their warm, tree-top utterance. The blackbird is beyond our praise; his threnody, his exquisite long phrases; his slow, tender lapses into self communing, have in June an almost intolerable beauty. He thinks of God, and sings loud and clear to the faint sky and the limp, scented leaves. Then he thinks of his love—his nesting love, mute and still as a stone in her round, secret nest, and a marvellous quietude

comes into the song.

All the warblers are singing now, some almost as wonderfully as the nightingale, others so faintly that they are seldom heard, speaking in a sibilant whisper like the long-tailed tit. The blue-tit and the chiff-chaff begin to declaim their dual and triple notes before it is light, and the larks are singing before the sun is up.

Now you may hear the blackcap's lovely voice, and the hoarse corncrake, whose rasp in the deep clover-scented grass is as full of magic as are the harsh cawing of rooks, the cynical laughter of grouse, the loud, uncontrolled merriment of the woodpecker. The robin, gorged and resplendent, is singing; so is the wren, though more noticeable later in the year.

The little brown dove has arrived and purrs from the high hedges all day with slumberous content. On the hills the curlews startle the air with sudden silver; in the turnip fields, by moonlight, the lapwings call; along the brooks dippers break into song as fresh and clear as a fountain. The owls, confused by the early light, send a long halloo shuddering through the gay chorus, and the yellow-hammer, with the perseverance of a limited intelligence, insists upon 'a little bit of bread and *no* cheese!'

In June dawns birds will sometimes forget the reserve of the wild, and will share one's breakfast as a robin once shared mine daily, singing very mellifluously from the butterdish after a cool meal of yellow butter. But he would not sing at all for margarine, only shaking his head a little, and wiping his beak insultingly upon the grass, and beadily staring, as if to say: 'The singer is worthy of something better than mere margarine.'

Towards the end of the month the birds are so gorged with good things that they simply *cannot*

sing. All spring Nature has kept a good table,
but now, what with the currants and the straw-
berries, the wall-fruit and the cherry orchards,
there is such a feast that they have a real orgy.
After all they have sung their songs, woven their
nests, led out their eager young. It is time to
feast, and feast they do, from the fading of the
dawn star to the rising of the evening star. Even
then, in the late dews, they will make music for
us, and all through July the swallows—tenderest
of June rhapsodists—keep up their sweet chatter,
long-drawn and poignant, full of some mysterious
vague sorrow, some augury of unrest which is
the slow magnetic pull of Africa.

"JOHN HALIFAX, GENTLEMAN"

Mrs. Craik's Green Twilights and Sunday Bells

DINAH MARIA MULOCK, afterwards Mrs. Craik, was born at Stoke-on-Trent on April 20, 1826. It is pleasant, to one coming from a sister county, to think that a bunch of country primroses probably stood by her mother's bedside.

Maria Mulock was to develop a deep and sincere love for the beauty of her own gentle landscapes, and to describe those woods and fields with a charm which sometimes reminds one of Miss Mitford's, and with a restraint which is occasionally like that of George Eliot's. Simplicity and restraint are her key-notes, and are probably the reason why her novel has been so much liked by the rank and file, the quiet, humdrum, unemotional people who do so much of the world's work.

But she was not without a capacity for controlled passion, as she once or twice shows in her hero, John Halifax. This may have been because she was not altogether Saxon, but one of those compounds of two races which so often excel in the arts.

Her father is described as 'an eccentric religious enthusiast of Irish extraction.' This would seem to indicate that the family life would not be tedious. Nevertheless, by the time she reached the age of twenty, Maria Mulock had had enough of it, and came to London with the determination to make her own living by writing. One must not forget that in those days, only ten years after Victoria's accession, this was a most original and unusual thing to do, a thing she probably would not have done but for that dash of the Celt.

She spent eighteen years in literary work, beginning with children's stories. No doubt, after the manner of her time, she felt that her immature work was good enough for children, and indeed they must have welcomed her *naïveté* and freshness after the 'Cautionary Tales' and such stuff to which they were inured.

She seems to have experimented with most types of literature, and to have produced the same kind of books which we get from the ordinary woman writer to-day. She wrote 'A Woman's Thoughts about Women,' which, no doubt, was the Staffordshire side coming out, for it is prosaic for a woman to write her general thoughts about her own sex. It is prosaic to think much about women unless one is a man, when it is usually wrong! But one gathers that she would have considered it most undesirable and not a little improper to write her thoughts about men —except impersonally, in a novel.

She wrote accounts of tours in Ireland and Cornwall, short stories ('Avillion and Other Tales') and lyrics. This last venture was more original than we realize, unless we remember that ladies in Miss Mulock's young days treated their lyrical outbursts as secret sins, and had them printed privately. But her main output was the novel. She wrote 'The Ogilvies' (1849), 'Olive' (1850), 'The Head of the Family' (1851), 'Agatha's Husband' (1853). She waited till 1857 to write her masterpiece—'John Halifax, Gentleman,' a book which in its solid worth, artistic integrity and leashed power is so good that one cannot imagine how it missed being a great book, a work of genius.

Certainly John is a better character, in so far as he goes, than is Charlotte Brontë's Rochester. If he had gone further, she would have fared better and become a classic. But her conventionality was a little too much for her art. Yet John did not often fail. What could be better than his sudden, almost savage, kissing of his love's wounded hand—his rich lady-love, and he a poor man? Only, could he have 'gone the next moment'? And once again, relentlessly, Miss Mulock would have dismissed him for a reason which we sensibly realize now was no reason, only her heroine rebelled. (The dash of the Celt had much to answer for, good luck to it!) And then, in seven lines, Maria Mulock did reach genius.

'It was but a low, faint cry . . . but he heard it, felt it . . . he took her into the shelter of his love for evermore.' That is the essence of it. You cannot read that paragraph, and the line about Jael bringing the lights, 'all in a wild dazzle,' without a stir of the pulses. You cannot read it without knowing that when Maria Mulock married, at the late age of thirty-eight, Mr. Craik of Macmillans, it was no shrewd move on her part, calculated to help on her books. A woman who could create John Halifax would not condescend to that. No. Whatever Craik seemed to the office staff of that distinguished house, whether or not he were 'self made' (which are we not all, so help us God!), whether he were long and lean or short and stout, Methodistical or Pickwickian, Tory or Radical, practical or dreamy, he was, above all, a man, with something stalwart, invincible, unbuyable in him, with, also, that faint hauteur, inherited from Adam, the hauteur of the chief dynamic force in the world. At any rate, she thought so, or she would not have accepted him. 'Don't reason with me,' says John to his love; 'you cannot judge—you do not know.'

Reading this book, a mature mind must own that Maria Craik had greatness. John's short sentences are really fine.

' "This will not do," said John.' The world would be a poor place but for this tiny sentence with its terrific import. The manhood of the world, confronted by cruelty, injustice, filth, lies and intolerance, says, after due consideration, 'This will not do.' We have, then, a slave war, or some other war, or a revolution, or world peace. We step forward and God-ward.

The point is that when John Halifax says 'This will not do,' you may smash him into little bits before he will revoke his verdict. And because he is so strong he is also tender. With a final flash of inspiration Mrs. Craik does more for his personality than any description could do, for when he dies the life of the woman who loves him ebbs away. She has no words such as Cleopatra's:

'How shall I live out this great gap of time
  My Antony is away?'
She simply dies.

Now, at the centenary of Maria Craik, I, for one, should like to hail her, with her quiet grey landscapes, green twilights, Sunday bells, mild autumn mornings and polished, prim interiors, as a fine psychologist and a true woman.

THE POETRY OF THE PRAYER BOOK

Phrases that Touch Perfection: Folklore of the Soul

WHATEVER may be our position in regard to the Church, whether we take a mid-course or are at either of the extremes—communicants or agnostics—whether we are churchwardens or (as a pedlar once described himself to me) 'more of an outside prop than an inside pillar,' we must all agree as to the poetic beauty of the Liturgy. With some exceptions, its phrases almost touch perfection, especially those in the order for Evening Prayer.

Whether or not we believe all that the Prayer Book says, whether, even, we believe in a personal God, still the inspired prayers of this wonderful book can comfort us. For we can pray in many different ways. Some people, to use a common illustration, pray like a man sending a telephone message from one definite place to another. He and the recipient know about the message, and the desired result is achieved. Others pray like someone launching a wireless message into space. Where it will go he cannot guess. Who will pick it up, how many will hear it, who will reply to it, how long it will go on echoing away and away into the dark—all this is unknown to him. But does his message fail to be heard on that account? Surely not! Whoever is waiting for it will get it.

So those who do not agree with any special dogma can still, looking into the evening west, say, 'Lighten our darkness!' though they may have no idea what manner of Lord it is to whom they appeal, or whether they will get into touch only with some immense vital force which waits for their small vital force to find it.

Whether they pray like this or in the more definite manner of our fathers, at a set time, in a solid building, to a distinctly visualized and local wrought the Liturgy—with others—yet the metal

God, seems to affect the main issue very little. The important thing is that here are we, very small and blind and weak, wandering we know not whence, come from some dim, forgotten home and bound for an unglimpsed country, and our hearts 'burn within us,' and we weep like lost children.

'An infant crying for the light,
And with no language but a cry.'

These ancient prayers help us to be articulate. They express our own souls for us. The best of them express not only one nation, one age, but all, as do the best utterances of every creed. The desert chief, out-gazing the vesper star with his hawk eye, praising Mahomet with his stern lips, could, without any discordance, add, as one courteous chief to another, while the swift African night enfolded him: 'Lighten our darkness!' The little Chinese girl, hastening home, panic-stricken, through the pine forests of Kwan Lun, her paper lantern extinguished by a sudden storm, could, without offence to Confucius, murmur: 'Lighten my darkness, I beseech thee, oh Lord!'

The best of our prayers are, then, universal. That is because they have grown slowly, by gradual accretion, like rock strata and coral islands, and it is also because they have grown upwards from below, not downwards from the educated. For though sudden flashes of individual genius reveal the race-mind, yet as a rule we find that the great religious forms of prayer, English, Catholic or Greek, have grown gradually, as folk music does, and legend, and public opinion as to right and wrong.

So, although Cranmer was the goldsmith who wrought the Liturgy—with others—yet the metal had been accumulating for centuries. He had the *King's Primer* and other primers, and he had the scattered poetry of Tindale's Bible. He had the *Bidding Prayer*, which had grown, like the songs of trouvères, from generation to generation. Indeed, one might call these priests of the dim ages, with their churches lost in remote forests, in mountains, marshes and sea-marges, speaking from memory to a few worshippers prayers old as time almost, one might fitly call them God's trouvères. And when Cranmer, with reverent hand, took up and used these things, he was in direct touch with the deepest life of the race.

What lament unspoken, agonies unseen, hunger and thirst, long years of waiting for the beloved unreturning, wanderings, ecstasies, startled glimpses of a beauty beyond things seen are to be found gleaming and darkling in these pages! How modern the antique phrases are, as the ancient moon that is for ever young. What more cosmopolitan, what more communal than such sentences as, 'Our common supplications,' 'with one accord,' 'Our Father!' 'Have mercy upon all men,' 'Give us this day our daily bread'?

Does a woman watch, pale and wild, for husband or son? She may hear, as no doubt in the Wars of the Roses she might have heard, through the churches' open windows, her men being commended to the 'fatherly goodness.' Has someone had the silent, final intimation, 'All is over'? He or she may hear, 'Unto God's gracious mercy and protection we commit thee. The Lord bless thee and keep thee. The Lord make His face to shine upon thee and be gracious unto thee. The Lord lift up His countenance upon thee and give thee peace.' Or is someone steeped in evil, sinking in its horrible quicksands? Let him hear the voice of humanity rolling down the ages, '*In Te, Domine, speravi; non confundar in æternum.*'

Or do the silver trumpets sound for love? It is all there, in the old mysterious book, in a score or so of words, strong and tender. 'With this ring I thee wed. With my body I thee worship.' '. . . to have and to hold, from this day forward, for better, for worse, for richer, for poorer, in sickness and in health, to love and to cherish.'

What more perfect words could be found for splendid manhood, so eager with his heart and his 'worldly goods,' his head and his hand, his dreams and his life to lay at her feet? What better words than those here for womanhood with her simple gift of surrender?

And all these, from the '*non confundar*' to the plighting of the troth, are ours, whether we go to church or not. They were bequeathed to us by hundreds of thousands of wistful people in many ages, of many manners, often troubled, often mistaken, often quaint and bigoted and harsh, but always greatly desiring loveliness and right-eousness. The Prayer Book is ours by divine right, because it is the folklore of the soul.

A PEDLAR OF LEAVES

HE IS always to be seen, whatever the weather, at his windy corner in that rather forlorn street which he brightens with his basket. He shakes with palsy as much in summer heats as in winter frosts; and well he may! For every morning, before the dawn, he is away into the dank, sparse meadow lands that ring London and give a pale, distorted reflection of the country. He walks for half the night, and when the first whiteness comes in the east he wades into the icy winter swamps for cresses, or stands knee-deep in the rimy grass to gather branches of early sallow, or adventures into the sobbing, forbidden woods for the first primroses. At Christmas, with fortune on his side, he may find a tree of well-berried holly or even a bunch of mistletoe, which he will wrest from some rich man's apple-tree in the eerie hours before the day. In July he has, among his wild posies, lavender. He sings the Lavender Song, old and fragrant.

'Won't you buy my sweet, bloomy lavender?'

In May he has a treasure-trove of king-cups.

'King-cups for May Day! Beautiful king-cups! Fine, fresh king-cups for the little ladies!'

There are times of scarcity when he has nothing but groundsel. Those are bad times, for the folk who like groundsel are a small, caged company, and cannot go flying down the streets to buy as much as they would like. Still he is not discouraged. He meets the limited demand for groundsel with skill and tact based on sound psychology. He waits till the day is aired, and there begin to come by his corner old ladies bringing with them an atmosphere of warm rooms full of indiarubber plants, wool mats, and canaries. These he singles out with a powerful, magnetic, though rheumy grey eye. He does not ask them to buy. He simple says, in a voice of mingled cajolery, pleading, authority, and badinage—

'The little birds!'

Whatever else he has or has not, there are always leaves in his basket In autumn he has great sheaves of them, a real booth of branches, rosy elder, tender pale-golden aspen, bronze beech. Then there is such a rustling at the windy corner that you would think a fairy forest grew there, or the tree of life, springing out of the pavement. In spring he has wych elm just bursting into bud, and tasselled larch, and the ethereal leafy traceries of birch.

His hands shake and shudder like aspen leaves, and make a rustling among his boughs on the stillest day. You would think, seeing him shake so, that he could never guide the pennies into his pocket, nor last the day out. Yet he does, and the year too, and other years, that rustle about him like his leaves. His long hair, his long beard, of the colour of bleached sphagnum moss, are unbelievably theatrical, beneath

a hat which was once a parson's. His coat and his ancient boots are not so much like cloth and leather as lichen. One feels, meeting his dauntless eye, realizing that he has never known comfort or ease or a sufficiency, that he will patiently stand there for ever, as he seems to have stood for aeons already. Can the day ever dawn when the leaf of that courageous life will be fallen? One would rather think that on some dark spring morning, with the fields white-over and a missel-thrush uttering a note or two beneath his breath, our friend will adventure with his reckless, jubilant boy's heart, a little further than his wont, and so, with a burden of beauty lisping about his head, gently blunder into immortality.

REVIEW ARTICLES
The Bookman

MORTON LUCE

Morton Luce, poet, scholar and friend of the finest minds among his contemporaries, is known and loved by the discerning, but his retiring temperament and his almost hermit life have kept him from being as well known as he ought to be to the general public. Remote from London, between the blue sea and the purple hills, he dwells 'where there are few to praise,' but where, surely, all who meet him must be aware of the dignity and beauty of a personality which could so well have sustained an equal friendship with Wordsworth, and which would certainly have given that poet help in some of those metrical lapses to which even great men are prone. For one of Morton Luce's gifts is his delicate perfection of form, and it is this which makes his 'Thysia' one of the most exquisite English sonnet-sequences. To express great and devastating emotions through the severe medium of the sonnet would be almost impossible to a modern mind, which loves to wander in lush, untrammelled ways. But it is typical of the best minds of the Victorian age. This is, I think, because the Victorians believed in reserve, control, abnegation, and rather mistrusted lavishness and freedom. In fact, if you could have set before a literary Victorian in his youth some of the free verse that is produced to-day I think it would almost have killed him. Of course perfection of form has its drawbacks, it does sometimes result in the loss of spontaneity and accuracy of idea. There were Victorians who would, if the rhyme so required, substitute 'like' for 'love,' and if their poem about, let us say, a tacamac poplar, proved difficult, would light-heartedly substitute the vague, unsatisfactory 'tree,' or would in desperation call it a Lombardy poplar, or even 'aspen.' Mr. Luce never does these things because his emotional power and his love of nature are great enough to stand the test of metrical perfection. In his nature poetry, with which alone I wish to deal now, he has both accuracy and spontaneity, gifts much rarer in his youth than they are now. It is these, combined with beauty of manner, that lead one to compare his work with things like 'The Lady of Shalott' and 'The Scholar Gipsy,' which, to my mind, are fitter companions for his poems than anything of Crabbe's, though it is easily seen why he has been compared with one who, while being his inferior as a poet, is his equal in the close observation and vivid visualisation of nature. But whereas Crabbe is always pedestrian, Morton Luce is very seldom so, and at his best he can express the simplest, homeliest things with genius. He can create, from what to some minds would be a commonplace stroll over a dull bit of marshy land, so keen a loveliness that it cuts one to the heart:

'Of creatures rare, elfin, mysterious,
Of aromatic sheen and scented gloom . . .
And all sweet peril of dim ways untrod.'

What a marvellous line that last is, and how we should all quote and requote and go crazy over it if Tennyson had written it! And what fools we are, to let fair souls live unheeded among us just because their names do not happen to have been said or shouted a sufficient number of times for us to dare to commit ourselves. Who strewed flowers for Mangan or Beddoes or Richard Middleton? Yet did the belauded Browning often write anything that could even remotely compare with 'Dream Pedlary,' or 'The Nameless One,' or Middleton's tender lullaby, 'You'll be my Baby now'?

Here is another magical couplet, from Mr. Luce's poem called 'A Rookery':

'And elfin shadows flitted round the boles,
And white beams crept along enchanted
                                    ground.'

Here also he speaks of 'The secret blossoms of the hazel,' which has that inexplicable quality of the phrases of genius. Why 'secret'? One does not know. They are under the leaves, but so are those of many trees. But one has come near to the hazel through its new mystery. And in another poem he says:

'The lane ascends
Through balmy hummings.'

Immediately we know the lane—deep, warm, overgrown with flowers—pale and very sweet—strown with the white wild cherry, blessed by the speedwell, so remotely fair. If he had not chosen to tell us of these things we should have had them by virtue of that one line, and I wonder if anyone has expressed the golden-dripping wonder of the lime better than in this same poem:

'. . . a lime,
That hangs its boughs with budded
                              murmurings.'

Of all the lovely things in 'New Idyllia,' the following is, I think, my favourite:

'Harbours where lilies anchor, pools which
                                    spread
Their dark metallic silver under boughs
That hide the sullen pike. Then to the beds
Of the rose-purple willow-herb that floods
Out from the brink its own far-billowing tide
Wondrously fair; and next by oozy groves
Of flag and osier, where from some green spray
Nigh to his mate (coy glancing from the deep
Seclusion of her blossom-broidered nest
That hangs 'twixt sky and wave) the reed
                                    warbler
Trills a quaint melody.'

And another from the same poem well bears out the author's own statement, in an essay on the nature-painting of Shakespeare, that so simple a thing as a list of flowers may be very fine poetry:

'Loosestrife and meadowsweet and marigold
And iris bright; and on their hedgerow banks
(Gay with the wealthiest garland of the year)
The deep blue Summer bellflower, vanquishing
All primal beauty of the hyacinth,
And foxgloves danced about by fan-winged
                                    flies,
Azure of cranesbill, and the ruddy gem
Of woodbine, and the purple-jewelled bud
Of scabious, lovelier than the open flower.
Their acres of live gold; their leagues of rose;
Roods of moon daisies over which the dusk
Draws not her veil.'

And it is not only in painting sheer beauty, such things as 'The mellow haw, faint elder, dewberry,' that Morton Luce excels. He is equally happy in depicting the macabre, and this is probably one reason why he has been compared to Crabbe. Is not the essence of desolation in:

'A wild waste sea beating on wasted land'?

And of autumn in:

'The last pale apple to the ground was
                              hurled . . .'?

And here also:

'Bare was the glebe, the rick cloth furled;
The swallow mustered for his flight;
Then cold mist filled the silent world,
And she was hidden from my sight.'

And again:

'Ah me, the year is growing old,
And sick withal, and numb with grief;
Drear is the stubble; from the wold
No song of bird; the weary leaf
Falls through the stagnant air, and dies;
The dormouse finds his living tomb;
Only where one last sunbeam lies
The drone dreams in the ivy bloom.'

The most concentrated poem of natural desolation is the one called 'A Windmill.' Why do so many people dislike windmills? Morton Luce, Beatrice Kean Seymour, Martin Armstrong have all three painted windmills in the most grievous colours. One could understand it if it were a water mill; but a high, sunny, breezy windmill! Why should that give such a gloomy impression? As for the Dutch windmills, with their bright colours, their business, their numbers, they give an impression of almost hysterical cheerfulness. But Mr. Luce's windmill is not like that. And in spite of my partiality for mills of all kinds, his power of creating atmosphere is so fine that when I read that poem it always brings to me a sense of horror.

It is difficult in so short an essay to give an idea of the good things in the books of this most quotable of poets. One longs to put things in wholesale. But if any reader wants a charming companion on a summer holiday, let him take 'New Idyllia,' or 'Threnodies,' or 'Idyllia,' and he will find that the green haunts he visits will become infinitely more beautiful because of them, for they will have helped him to garner not only the colour and scent, but the very soul, the 'beauty beyond beauty' of:

'The last sweet bluebell and the first sweet
                                        rose.'

THE SOUL OF AUSTRALIA*

There is in the human heart a kind of love—spiritual, exotic and strange—which for lack of a better phrase may be called geographic passion. It is a mysterious emotion, little understood, more often to be found in men than in women, because the essence of nature is a large, calm passivity, and passivity is what man demands in his lover, whether woman or forest. This passion can be so intense and all-pervasive as to take the place of sex love, and it can be so dynamic as to devastate the life into which it comes. Nothing can satisfy the lover but absolute possession, so that there is something tragic and fated always about this passion, for it is a thing incalculable by any human mind, to have this lover's mastery over the innate mystery of the world, to compass with mortal arms the fugitive divine glory. For this is no common love of a wood or a meadow, but rather a seeking beyond all woods and meadows for the unique wonder which once, in some wild acre (for ever afterwards to us a hallowed acre), broke through and came to its lover like flame, like moonrise on the sea, like a tempest of butterflies or an angel singing on a mountain. Or it may come more sadly and starkly, calling so that home and hearth are deserted, offering bitter fruits which yet seem sweeter than apples of the known orchard. It is

* 'Daimon.' By E. L. Grant Watson. 7s. 6d. (Jonathan Cape.)

in fact what Grant Watson so well calls it—the 'daimon' of a place—and Grant Watson is one of the very few who can express it. Conrad could. His was the daimon of the sea. There is something in his long lagoons, his islands, low and jewelled, on the water, his faint tropic horizons in a mist of sleeping horror, which is not there when most people write of them. And so with Grant Watson and the Australian Bush. It is true that 'their being is to be perceived' and Grant Watson has not only seen objectively and subjectively, but he can also show his readers these strange pictures of fawn-coloured and grey wastes beneath immense and lovely skies, brooded over by who knows what dovelike or vulture-like presence.

'Daimon' is a remarkable book, but far more remarkable when considered as the third of a trilogy containing also 'The Desert Horizon' and 'Mainland.' For it is the cumulative effect which counts in work of this kind. It is impossible to express anything so almost beyond expression except with the vitality, the stamina which can build up its idea in book after book, so that one sees the vast continent unrolling, curve on curve, plain on grey plain; sees the solemn gods of cloud pass in slow majesty; hears the surge of the wind in the low forests with the certainty, the thoroughness of lifelong knowledge.

In these three books Grant Watson has caged something that waited out there in the wild, grey bush, invisible, intractable, yet desiring to be found, to be enshrined, but which could not have been shown to us in just this way without this one special mind as its medium. The bush and the spirit of it come to one subtly all through 'Daimon,' and one becomes aware, as also in 'Mainland' and 'The Desert Horizon,' of something which one may describe as a vast and mighty silence pressing in upon the spirit.

Now it is a rare gift to be able to perceive and interpret these mysteries, to be able not only to describe but to create living characters and to portray through them the vast misty protagonist beyond the book. It is a great thing to do this, even if it takes a lifetime. But Grant Watson is young. He has done this or at least begun to do it in three novels. He has done it strongly yet

subtly, with a ruggedness which can turn to a fragile sweetness.

Grant Watson has a future and is, it seems to me, the one among the young Englishmen now writing who is most likely to prove to be the worthy successor of Conrad.

HELEN PROTHERO LEWIS*

'THE HILL BEYOND'* is the fifteenth novel written by Helen Prothero Lewis, and though it has not the charming setting of 'Love and the Whirlwind' and the others which have Welsh landscapes for their background, it shows no decline in the essential qualities of its authoress, which are charm, simplicity, humour, courage, love of beauty, both human and natural, and the gift of weaving a romance. A large circle of readers have discovered this gift of hers, and love to sit at her feet and forget their troubles and pains and businesses in the allure of her happy stories. She deserves her large public, her big sales and good reviews, for she has a real talent which she has honestly and sincerely cultivated and developed. Sometimes there are sentences, bits of description, flashes of intuition, especially in the romances of the country-side, which make one think that, had she been less normal, less conventional, the authoress might have written something in the vein of 'Wuthering Heights.' There are some macabre touches in 'Love and the Whirlwind,' where the brooding atmosphere of approaching catastrophe which surrounds the

* 'The Hill Beyond'. 7s. 6d. (Hutchinson.)

two dark, wild brothers is very well done. Of all her qualities the most outstanding is a quiet, unaffected humanity.

Mr. de la Mare once propounded to me the conundrum—'What is it that best-sellers and geniuses sometimes have in common, which holds the imagination of the everyday reader?' I hazarded: 'Humanity.' You never find a cold book becoming popular. Pater will always be caviare, so will Ibsen and Strindberg and Croce, while the name of Charles Dickens goes round the world like a caress. The ordinary person does not mind moralisings or trite sayings or clichés, he does not even mind their exact opposite—genius; but he cannot bear frigidity. He must have warmth and comfort. He is afraid of the infinities. He desires what Sir Edmund Gosse so beautifully sums up in his phrase, 'the ecstatic human.'

Now Helen Prothero Lewis, in her own personality and in her books, always recalls to me this phrase. And this quality, although she would be the last to arrogate to herself any claim to genius, yet makes her of the company of such as Dickens, while many with genius as great as his cannot, we feel, be classed with him at all. The ecstatic human always thinks that humanity *means* well even if it does not *do* well. Helen Prothero Lewis believes this, and so her books are a rest cure. One knows that there will be no agonised uncontent with God and all His works; no red gashes of lust startling up from the beast of long ago; no spiritual savageries like Dante's; not a vestige of that blank horror which is the hell of genius. We are not on the Alps of the soul now—the fierce, God-tormented mountain, where only stars are our company, and the flare of them kills the heart. No. We are in a garden, a quiet, walled garden where, even in rough times, a lady might walk at ease, not fearing the loud voices of the men-at-arms. Pleasant trees make a shelter from the storm. The fruit hangs ripe, and is not torn untimely from the bough. The well tended flowers are long in bloom, not blighted nor broken. The birds are wise and circumspect, and even the insects—most bloodthirsty of created things—are careful to wear their least cannibal expression. It is delightful to walk in this garden with its kindly châtelaine, meeting heroines who

are lovely and good, who say their prayers, are bashful, can blush, and are not afraid to confess that they cannot sing or play without their portfolios; old men who are reverend and revered; young men who, though one may find them slightly etiolated, are yet free from the 'smut' and other unpleasant attributes which less pure-minded writers cannot help seeing in the modern man. That the characters are too 'true to type' ever to emerge completely from their background is immaterial. We do not *want* them to emerge. It is peaceful to know that they will stop there, like tapestry figures, and that never shall we receive the shocks that Life can give. For Life, with a laugh like a neigh, will reveal the boy with the beautiful poetic face as a mass of obscenity, and the strong silent man as a secret drug-fiend, and will show us a mother betraying her child, and a woman like an angel poisoning her lover. 'There is your material!' says Life. 'Now let the genius use it.' And the unhappy genius produces from his harrowed soul unclean and horrible creatures, and goes mad; and a clammy finger of madness is on all who read. (But somehow, in the terror, we stumble a little nearer to God.)

After this, what a rest to hear the robins in Helen Prothero Lewis's garden lisping, 'Whatever is, is well!' and her thrushes singing, 'God's in His heaven!' We feel as a man might who had been wrestling with waste land amid the fury of the elements and was invited to rest in an orangery, there to walk or to recline, with fruit to hand and just enough sun, and pleasant shade.

Whatever the sorrows and perplexities of her Dorindas and Susans, even though they include deception, as in the story, 'As God Made Her,' the reader is secure in the knowledge that 'All shall be well, and all manner of things shall be well.'

Susan, in 'The Hill Beyond,' will extricate herself from the arms of Bruce, her fiancé, and subside into the arms of Walter (whose wife the authoress gets rid of in a perfectly unexceptionable way) and will come with music and acclamation to the haven where she would be. But in real life the Susans so often do not know what their haven is, and if they do know, wives refuse to be expunged, and Susan, though Walter gives her 'the world to walk on,' yet loves Bruce best, but is fascinated by Walter, so that she sometimes earns that most catholic of sobriquets—immoral —and is not Helen Prothero Lewis's white and guarded Susan at all, but a more complex, more interesting being. But this is the essence of romance—that the Susans find their Walters, the tweeny-maids become great ladies, the accused murderer is acquitted because somebody else's bullet arrived first. The last occurs in 'Love and the Whirlwind,' when Griffith shoots at his brother and it is only found out afterwards that an angry poacher had the same idea and a better aim. But one cannot help feeling that this accident could not clear Griffith of his murderous intention.

But again, this is what romance should be. The great romantic writers, like rosy-fingered gods and goddesses, mould the ancient scheme of things afresh, paint it with rainbow lights, and create something 'nearer to the heart's desire.' We should probably not like it if we had it—this world hedged with blossomed may, with white butterflies, wing to wing, guarding the gates, with white-clad knights to ride forth in immortal youth to kill dragons at dawn, and return in the evening without a spot or crease on their garments, but with the defiant dragon on their saddle bow—or wherever it is you put trophies of this kind. It is nice to read of it. It is nice for Susan, while she muddles along, to think, 'If I wasn't me, I could have a life like this which Helen Prothero Lewis has sketched.' But all the time she knows that her personality can only develop by muddling along.

The management of plot in these novels is usually very good. The plots are often intricately woven, and though they do not come out of the characters, yet they often give an impression of doing so. The element of surprise is very skilfully used. This again is essential romance—that, in the humdrum of life, something strange and wonderful should happen—a gift fall from the sky, flowers bloom in the snow, dawn shine at midnight. Humanity is the ragged child outside the pastrycook's window. Philanthropy gives it a plain bun. Romance gives it a sugar cake. And though it could not live on sugar cakes they do its soul good.

Last but not least, Helen Prothero Lewis loves nature. She has some charming pastels in word-painting, especially in the Welsh novels. There are some in 'The Rudder and the Rock,' I believe, about the Minehead country; but I have not been able, so far, to read that, being stopped on the first page thus:

'There is thrown in, two or three times a week, the chase of the wild red deer . . . it is enough . . . the sight, be it but a glimpse, rewards.' It was enough for me. I want to see Helen Prothero Lewis on the side of mercy, and not on the side of those who kill for pleasure.

But she can describe 'the exquisite purple light on far-away hills, at eventide.' And she can describe the sea, and get into her description something of the sea-murmur, and the tonic of ozone. Pine-woods, also, she can bring to mind, and spinneys in the valleys, and mountain streams, heathery summits, purple table-lands. It can well be said of her, as she says of one of her characters:

> 'She felt the spell of wild mountains, heard the rush of wild winds sweeping down wild valleys, saw the processions of the white-robed bards chanting wild melodies to the skies.'

She only needs to feel a little more deeply the nature-ecstasy, the 'hiraeth,' to do really fine work of this kind, for one feels that the rapture, the passion, the grief of the mountains are in her soul and only need expression.

CONTRAST*

Pᴵᴄᴛᴜʀᴇ papers, printing charming portraits of authors, weaken a reviewer's hand. How can one slate Mr. Moss for his too facile pen, chit-chat, the general unnourishing airiness of his cream when, in *T.P.'s Weekly*, he has such a quizzical, disarming smile, as if saying, 'I am bigger than this.' He *is* bigger. Once he wrote a fine, stark, tragic story about a woman who so much longed to go home that she became a prostitute for one night to earn the fare: but the exchange altered, and it was not enough. Because he can write thus, he has no right to waste time in describing silly parties, mushy society, people with grand names and nothing else, the 'comedy of manners' which is only tolerable when on the stage, and even then must be created by a master and must not last too long. The only character claiming our sympathies is the General's, and that is more for what we know he did in the past than for anything Mr. Moss says of him. His way of saying 'ter' for 'to' and 'yer' for 'you' is not convincing. On those rare occasions when one has been fortunate enough to converse with a General, he did not do this. Again, if his wife gave to another the passion she had never given him, I do not think a soldier would have taken it like this. Either he would in the old-fashioned way have 'seen red' and shot everybody, or he would, in the newer way, have seen that there was much in his wife's personality which he could not understand or satisfy, and would have been content without fuss to let their relationship remain as it was. But then comes the question,

* 'Hangman's House.' By Donn Byrne. 7s. 6d. net. (Sampson Low.)—'Whipped Cream.' By Geoffrey Moss. 7s. 6d. net. (Hutchinson.)

would he ever have cared for such a person as Lindy—that irritating little fool, selfish, deceitful, felinely feminine, who wanted whipping instead of the cream? I beseech Mr. Moss to write again of real people, because he is too real to succeed in anything else.

I have seen no portrait of Donn Byrne. No disarmament is necessary here. His book enslaves. From the first page to the last (except for two sins—D'Arcy's cruel end and the fox-hunting) we listen breathlessly as folk of old to the troubadours; we are as hungry for more as a nestful of fledgelings. I said, 'I will not fall under the spell of this fox-hunting Irishman, though T. P. O'Connor says he is a genius, and T. P. O'Connor is generally right.' Frigid, I read the foreword, began the first page, and was there unwittingly and utterly thawed by the misuse of a pronoun!

'The primroses,' says Donn Byrne, '*who* should have been gone.'

So he is a true son of earth, not 'an hireling.' He participates, shares the sacrament; sees eye to eye with the daisy; leans with the larch in storm; kisses the rose on the mouth; shudders up to the light with the earliest leaf. It is a surprisingly small company, that of the true children of earth, in a world where everybody talks of 'love of nature,' everybody writes 'nature books,' everybody is 'fond of the country.'

(If you are a child of earth you are not 'fond' but impassioned, devastated, recreated by these things. You are often terrified, your soul faints within you, you are driven into the wilderness. It is not an easy way. Nature is not a kind mother, and whom she loves she chastens.)

Donn Byrne is of that company. Hence the vividness of his pictures, which have the lucent intense colour of landscapes on a gleamy May day. 'More gold than gloom of the broom . . . redder than reddest rose,' says the Mabinogion of my ancestral country, which always seems to be kin to some of the ancient Irish books. The Celt must write like this, because his heart is breaking with its garnered beauty, his eyes are blinded with vision. Therefore the control of Donn Byrne's treatment of these things is the more wonderful. One knows that he has seen the world kindle to a white heat; melt in a mist of ecstasy. That for him colour surges like blue veins in a sea wave, like spring's blood leaping in a petal of wild apple. Everything is triple-distilled. Everything is in essence. Listen!

'The turf that burns with the deep red of rubies, and has a terrible nostalgic scent to it, of the crisp grass and of white bog flowers, and of great forests forgotten. . . .'

'The queer, soft alighting of birds.'

'The foggy dew still rested, so that the kine and horses were breast deep in it, as in a sea of silver.'

'Five of the clock, and darkness in it, and a little white frost creeping out.'

And the description of Connaught coming to her lover in a boat, and how 'a long wave murmured before it,' is like a bit from the old Greek. But one of the finest things is the account of the race, and the bird that ran across the track:

'His loud, fearsome chirrup rose quaintly above the thumping of the hoofs.'

Donn Byrne has ridden in a race, or he would never have put that in. It is wonderfully vivid.

But in the matter of fox-hunting I wish I were a witch to cast a spell on him and lure him to a tall haunted mountain I know, nearly two thousand feet nearer God than most folks' dwellings. Then I would turn him into a little red fox with anxious amber eyes and a very quick, troubled pulse, and hear the scattered notes of questing hounds and think, 'Teach him to glorify fox-hunting!' And then—why then, I should remember his really exquisite style and disenchant him just in time! Donn Byrne should have a future. He could write like a demon or a seraph. He might, in middle age, even write like a god.

'PLUS QUE DE L'ESPRIT'*

'ARIEL' was the first book by André Maurois that I had the good fortune to read. It gave a shock of joy, exquisite, like a sudden breath of sweetbriar on an April evening, for the prevailing impression given by the author's work is that of delicate elegance. The feeling for words, for '*le mot juste*,' is quite astonishing in these days, when wholly illiterate (though supposedly educated) people flounder desperately in their own tangled ideas, and pick up one word after another in the vain hope of cutting their way out, but with complete indifference to the most rudimentary meaning of the words. How charming, then, to find M. Maurois not only caring for the rudimentary meanings, but for the finest gradations, the faint implications, the sigh of an echo. It is this which enables him to achieve those epigrammatic sentences which come at the end of each chapter in 'Ariel,' which one awaits with never-disappointed hope, which sum up and fix everything in the previous chapter, which are almost always the direct result of a sudden flash of genius, giving to the book its character. This personality of the book and of his new book, 'Mape,' is at once very definite and very difficult to capture. A tenderness veiled with satire, a penetrating absorption hidden in apparent indifference. He is a most kind friend to his marionettes—who are yet so alive that we never regard them as marionettes—but there is not one of them, with the possible exception of Mary Shelley, whom he seems sorry to consign again to the box. For a little while the personality in its grace or silliness, decorous or swaggering, is alive under the hand of Maurois. Then, as if with

* 'Mape.' By André Maurois. 7s. 6d. (Bodley Head.)

a short, half-mocking laugh, he relinquishes it. His attitude is very much that of Browning in his poem beginning:

'And did you once see Shelley plain?'

The poem continues, with a non-Browningesque succinctness:

'But you were living before that,
And also you are living after.'

He is no hero-worshipper, nor does he write of humanity from the altitude of deity. He neither looks up nor down, but simply straight at people, and though he is not sufficiently a mystic to see right through them, into the innermost shrine where is a lamp or blackness, yet he is so keen, so acute, that he is able from the outward appearance of the shrine to tell us almost as much as the mystic could. His portraits of Mrs. Siddons and Mary Shelley are masterly. That type of woman is evidently a favourite with him, for he is so sympathetic in his delineation. The vein of practicality and common sense appeals to the shrewdness in his own character. In the case of Mrs. Siddons ('The Portrait of an Actress' in 'Mape') he has a person outside types—a woman beautiful, fêted, stirring passion, yet good; a genius who did not despise the cares of her rather stupid husband's house and table. In Mary Shelley he has the 'second fiddle,' which has always intrigued first-class intellects.

In 'Mape,' the study of Mrs. Siddons is by far the best. The first—'The Sorrows of Young Werther'—is a little too much of an incident to suit the author's style. A mature character, summed up by the actions of a lifetime, is his true theme. The second study, 'The Reader,' has a certain flatness about it, which perhaps it was difficult to avoid, since the dullard who, in his own life, copied the characters in books is the main character. But Mrs. Siddons calls out the same traits that so charmed us in 'Ariel.' What could be better than Mrs. Siddons accepting 'with professional tolerance' the threatened suicide of her daughter's lover? Or this:—'There is always great pleasure in a feeling of heroism, and vicarious heroism provides the purest form of it.' And the account of 'eyes that had not wept for forty years being suddenly able to shed veritable tears *as soon as the fashion had been*

established.' And the final *coup de grâce* which even the adorable Siddons does not escape. Maurois keeps it for the last sentence. He has described Mrs. Siddons, inconsolable after the loss of both daughters, finding relief for her passionate and suppressed grief in acting the parts of bereaved mothers. He describes her tears, her voice 'like a violin, breathing lamentation.' Then he says—'In the depth of her actress's soul a far-off melody, frail and almost gay, murmured again and yet again, "*I have never acted so well!*" '

La Bruyére said, '*Il faut plus que de l'esprit pour être auteur.*' M. Maurois has '*l'esprit*' and he has also a great deal else. His imagination is vivid and not, as is often the case with psychologists dealing with facts, stiffened and straitened. One guesses that if a fact were too troublesome he might tactfully quash it, but as a rule he triumphs over difficulties with which the purely creative mind never has to cope. He has invented a new kind of biography, far more fascinating than any other kind—biography in essence, plentifully salted with wit.

But perhaps, in all the galaxy of human beings long gone into the silence, creatures 'so bright and feyre,' but dead—till Maurois recalled them for a while—there is not one which interests us as much as does Maurois himself, Maurois in the noonday of his gifts, who may achieve even greater things yet.

THE WING OF PSYCHE*

Sᴇʟᴅᴏᴍ does the wing of Psyche brush the page of the philosopher, even fleetingly. He understands talent, intellect, will, the Napoleons, the statesmen, 'the kingdom, the power and the glory.' He understands a certain type of imagination. But the faint, far voice, the dew-dark wing athwart the dawn, he does not know. Mr. Wallas does know it or, rather, he glimpses it, which is all anybody can do. He says some most helpful and illuminating things about the creative mind, and especially the mind of the poet. The strange necessity for the subconscious, for using 'foreconscious processes for conscious ends,' is well understood. Only modern psychologists have begun to guess the all-importance of this dim waiting between the accomplishment of known fact and the sudden piercing awakening to what is beyond fact or thought. It is like the dark waiting on Easter morning. The experience is garnered, the life lived, the death died. What then? We wait by the sealed tomb for the clap of a wing, the sudden golden voice, the starting of immortality from its silent nest. It is the one thing needing. Having it, you may labour under every disadvantage, yet your work will be the work of genius. Not having it, take up golf, or croquet, or politics, but do not meddle with poetry. If you know much about your work—why you work, how you work, your aims—you are probably not a poet. The poet lets not his left hand know what his right hand doeth. He has little choice, little will. He is simply a listener on the shelving shores of the subconscious, hearing the mighty roar of far seas. How then shall he answer kind inquiries: 'How goes your book?' 'Are you working hard?' *Does* he ever work? What *has* he been doing, he wonders bemusedly, while publishers wait and friends look askance. Why, dear to goodness, he has only been listening to God! Does he work best in the morning or after lunch? Six hours a day, or more? 'Oh life, oh death, oh time!' He does not know. He has only been listening—listening to the mighty voice beyond the mountains, among the stars. Hardly ever does he do any conscious thinking. He listens; then he writes. Often he is greatly astonished at what he writes. But Mr. Wallas is not astonished. He understands. Very aptly he quotes a little girl who says: 'How can I know what I think till I see what I say?' Further says the author, whose humour is delightful: 'How can the most perfectly trained clergyman be sure that he will feel really sad at Tuesday's funeral or really joyful at Thursday's wedding?'

The effect of habit and the 'time-stimulus' on creative work is very competently discussed. So is the control of energy. In this chapter the effects of action and rest are contrasted. One would have liked to hear what Mr. Wallas has to say as to denial of normal desires—such for instance as the 'hiraeth' for Nature—and its effect on creative life.

Mr. Wallas is too well known to need my praise, yet I must thank him for this inspiring book. It is the work of a clear thinker who yet does not despise the vague meanderings of the imaginative writer. It is also the work of a mind which believes that physicists and physiologists will some day join hands with psychologists; which is almost tantamount to saying that God and matter are ultimately one.

---

* 'The Art of Thought.' By Graham Wallas. 7s. 6d. (Jonathan Cape.)

PILGRIMS OF ETERNITY*

A NY reader of Martin Armstrong's new book, 'Desert,' who happened to be acquainted with the author and his other books, will feel, on finishing this strange, fascinating story, not only admiration but bepuzzlement. For here is a dual personality. There are obviously two of Martin Armstrong. There is the rather boyish person who plays tennis, climbs mountains in Spain, and writes short stories and *contes* of modern life, psychological but not dramatic or visionary; who also wrote 'The Goat and Compasses,' with its vivid seascapes. But neither in this romance of modern life nor in the short stories was there anything to presage the other personality. This is the personality of a priest—possibly of a Trappist. Chill, severe, merciless to self and the senses, and to woman as temptress of the senses, it haunts the book, broodingly, without attempting to impose itself on the reader, yet quite unforgettably.

It is shown in the scene where the young man of fashion rushes from the over-scented, over-heated banqueting-hall, sated with the flesh, even at its rosiest and most delicate; in the picture of Helena, the rich courtesan; in the less carnal but still tempting emanation of the palm grove; in the fact that the only admirable woman in the story goes into a nunnery. But most it is shown in the character of Serapion, the old hermit, impervious to every mortal failing, every human desire, with his insistence on the doctrine, 'touch not, taste not, handle not, which all are to perish with the using.'

What a picture of negation it is when this hermit begins 'once more to draw the slender trail

of his footsteps onward still farther into the untrodden waste.' Why? Because 'the spirit driveth him.' He has reached, as the author says, 'the limit not only of humanity but of life itself.'

What a macabre, strongly imagined picture too of Malchus, athirst for a human voice in the great waste, wandering into a hermit's cave and placing his hands in friendship on the shoulders of a man seated there, only to find that the whole figure crumbles to dust at his touch. That expresses the monkish point of view in essence. So does the terrible last scene where Malchus seeks his lost, his lovely love. And coming through her garden—her once beautiful garden, waste now, and desolate, with only the rich rose laurels, the oleanders of Galilee, crimson, rosy and snow-white, passionately fragrant, blooming as of old—he reaches her room and sees (oh, horror worse than death!) sees his sweet love hideous and revolting, stricken with leprosy. He cries out that this is not his love, yet knows that it is, and so, stumbling blindly from the place of horror, he returns to the desert. His soul, sickened of material things, violently desires the approach of death, and 'hastens to be in futurity.'

In that chapter also is the monastic attitude.

All this, expressed with vividness and control, is remarkable in an author whose work has been typically modern, with the usual plot and setting. The thing which has been already noticeable in all his work and which is intensified here, is his power of giving, in a few sentences, vital pictures of Nature. Both in verse and prose he has this gift. His pictures have a crystal clarity, at once solid and malleable, reminiscent of the glass-green, apparently still water where it bends over a weir. Malachite, full of long spears of gold, shattering to a cool radiance of foam.

'The pure solitude wore the pale, flushed beauty of a flower.'

'The infinite grey desert lay dwarfed and shrunken beneath a vast sheaf of golden light.'

'From the blandest to the most sinister beauty, but always unreal, unearthly as some waste of the unpeopled moon.'

'The undulating immensity of bleached gold-dust.'

---

* 'Desert: a Legend.' By Martin Armstrong. 7s. 6d. (Jonathan Cape.)

'Flamingoes like long-stemmed rosy lilies
    dreaming immovably upon the fainter rose
    of their reflections.'
'Violet fissures' . . . 'snowy moonlight . . .'
One has it all, carved in high relief, painted in
rich colour. One can even breathe the sparkling
desert air.

The idea of antiquity is always present, though
there is no archaism in the language. One feels
that the soul of Serapion is as old, as terrible and
as indestructible as the desert which, in that far
century, dreamed as it dreams to-day, naked and
ghast beneath the eye of God. The antique feasts,
Theocritan shepherds, caravans, are depicted
without effort, yet a great deal of quiet work must
be at the back of this sureness of touch. In con-
sidering the book one recalls Anatole France
and 'Thäis.' Not that it is in any sense derivative.
It is too powerful for that. Having written it, the
author can never again be called merely brilliant.
It is touched with dark fire, and there are not
many young men of our day who could so
detach imagination from their own lives, 'survey-
ing eternity by that which is eternal in themselves.'

A POSY OF SWEET FLOWERS*

THERE is surely no more unselfish person than the
anthologist. For while all we others are
striving to ensure our own immortality with
eagerness, beguilements, buffooneries, loud voices,
'the sound of battle and garments rolled in
blood,' the anthologist is quietly ensuring the
immortality of somebody else. There is usually
no dreamer so unworldly as the anthologist. He
wanders in a vast garden, lost in wonder, unable
to decide often between flowers of equal loveliness. If he gathers a rose someone is sure to say
'Why did you not bring us violets?' If he lingers
near the lily, voices will clamour for sunflowers
or chrysanthemums. The true anthologist has the
greatest difficulty in finishing his book. There is
always just one more, a new, delicious discovery.
This I think is the way in which Wilfred Thorley
compiled his charming book. As to the way in
which the redoubtable Mr. Wotton—probably
our first anthologist—dealt with the material of
'A Hundreth Sundrie Flowres,' which he published in 1573, this cannot quite be said. For
Mr. Wotton was really too good a business man
to be a perfect anthologist. He was so very astute
that he could not have been at all dreamy. His
manner of entering the garden is rather that of a
brisk man with a sickle. Briskness was obligatory,
for if he could not get the thing finished before
the various wild-hearted, hot-headed, unwise

* 'A Bouquet from France.' By Wilfred
Thorley. 7s. 6d. and 10s. 6d. net. (Harrap.)—
'A Hundreth Sundrie Flowres.' 1 guinea and 2
guineas. (Haslewood Press.)

young men whose verse he was annexing returned from the Netherlands, they would probably object, and his anthology would come to nothing. So Mr. Wotton reaped with a will, and put in everything, even bits of love-letters which the unfortunate young men had written on the same pages as their poems, and which were intended simply for those fair ladies to whom they were indited. In they went! Away to the printers they were sent, and before the young soldiers returned, their inmost hearts were being discussed and enjoyed by the whole court. One does not hear that they did Mr. Wotton any physical damage. Possibly they trusted to their pen-names to disguise them. Possibly also the little god called 'ego' was pleased, in spite of Mr. Wotton's impudence, to see the poems in the glory of print. We also must be grateful to Mr. Wotton and to the editor and producers of this book, not only for the delightful manner of it—the real antique spelling in which those young gentlemen who fought for William of Orange expressed their loves and hopes—but also because there are so many charming verses here, and one or two really fine ones. 'Gascoigne's Lullabie' is a beautiful poem. The one 'In prayse of a Gentlewoman whose name was Phillip' is delicious. Why her name was Phillip, who she was, what she thought of the solemn fun of this song, are things we should like to know. As we cannot, let us take comfort in the reassurance of the couplet:

'Let others prayse what byrd they will,
Sweete Phillip shall be my byrd still!'

No doubt the fair Phillip was as pleased as the author hoped. The song beginning 'The stately Dames of Rome' is good in the ornate manner of that time, and there are others like it, full of pleasant conceits. Some of the shortest are the best. One very unusual and curious quatrain begins with the line:

'My mansion house was Mone: from
Dolor's dale I came'—

and is worth many of the longer ones. It is a fascinating book, beautifully printed and bound, and one cannot help agreeing with Mr. Wotton, when he says in his breezy, highhanded manner that 'if the authors object and other people are pleased,' he can claim 'to have gained a bushel of goodwill in exchange for one pint of peevish choler.' Kittle cattle, these authors! Mr. Wotton stands no nonsense. One wonders what the Author's Society would have said to him?

A 'Bouquet from France' contains some of the best lyrics of that land of exquisite poets. There are those one has always known, and there are new delights, such as Remy de Gourmont's lovely 'La Neige,' which I, for one, had never seen before. Heredia's sonnets about Cleopatra one is sorry to miss: but we have Victor Hugo's 'Retreat' and 'Solomon,' and Chénien's 'Chromis' and Lerberghe's 'La Mort,' and 'Sui je, sui je, sui je belle,' by Deschamps, and Ronsard's 'When you are old,' and the fresh loveliness of the thirteenth century anonymous poem, 'Within an Orchard.' There is too a perfect song by Marceline Desbordes-Valmore, 'La Couronne Effeuillée.'

The translations have the great merit of rendering the spirit of the poem. In actual wording they are sometimes rather free, as in the refrains of one or two which, whenever I have read them, have had no refrains. This seems to detract slightly from that severe simplicity which is the essence of the poems. Sometimes too the sense is obscured by the use of a word which is not the one absolute word. Thus the translator renders 'Il est des parfums frais comme des chairs d'enfants' as 'Some scents are chill as infants' flesh.' There is no one-syllabled word in English to express 'frais' in that context, except the literal 'fresh.' And one sees the difficulty of having 'fresh' and 'flesh' so near. But 'chill' is obviously wrong, bringing in the sense of marble statues and not of warm, live children. My only other criticism is of the too frequent use of the word 'Frore.' It is impertinent to criticise at all, when one has only intuition to light one, and not—as Mr. Thorley has—intuition allied with scholarship. But there is a way of catching the vibrations of the poet's soul, if one is in sympathy with him, by a kind of wireless, independent of language. And when one has done so, one is apt to forget that the translator has the weight of words to manipulate, and that although he has caught the inner meaning even more clearly than we, it is not always possible to get it on to paper.

But that Mr. Thorley can and does achieve this is shown by such intuitive flashes as 'frustrate rose' for 'la faute idéale des roses.'

The whole book, context and format alike, is a pleasure to handle and to look at, and the cover is charming. Wilfred Thorley is to be congratulated on his bouquet, gathered in the fragrant, ordered pleasaunces of France, in maytime and in dewtime, with its orchard bloom, its pinks and pansies, its roses of Provence and the deep-hearted purple lily of Heredia's genius.

'KNOWEST THOU THE LAND?'

IF ONLY Miss Sinclair would tell us where this village and all the other villages, deep drifted in magic, of which she writes, are to be found! Then we could steal away to them, not by train or motor, though, nor even by aeroplane, for they are not in Baedeker; they are in the Border Country that merges into the Beyond. Who would stay hereabouts if they could live in the house of Far End in the village of golden cottages drenched in golden light, terraced with sweetness of flowers in season, bells and cups, hoods and flags, scarlet gems and rosy bosses, submerged in petals of snow and flame, ivory and amaranth, argent and snapdragon-pink? The skies are tender blue there; the gales are warm, hawthorn-scented; the cupped tulips, stirless on their brittle stems, brim with light like goblets in the suave air. Could any house-agent find us so sunwarm, rose-cool a haven, what a fortune he would make!

We all have our dreams, but few dream so charmingly, paint so deliciously as Miss Sinclair.

*   'Far End.' By May Sinclair. 7s. 6d. (Hutchinson.)

A few sentences, with great economy of words, and the place is evoked. It is one of her great gifts to conjure the atmosphere of a place, whether of this golden village or of the ghast graveyard in 'Mary Olivier.' But she is most at home in the lovely places, in gardens where the limpid air blesses the dewy-eyed flowers; where lawns of close, fragrant turf take the blue, long shadows of ancient trees; where birds speak solace and fruits ripen on rosy walls. She has a clear, sweet sanity in her outlook on humanity which makes her work in tune with all these things. 'The fruits of the spirit are love, joy, peace.' After storm, calm weather. So she seldom has in her novels an unalleviated tragedy. Though in her treatment of evil she can be both subtle and severe, her general attitude to life is one of great simplicity. One misses the subtlety a little in this and kindred stories, but the *naiveté* is there still, the charity, the tenderness.

'Far End' is the story of a man who came back to his wife after an essay in merely physical passion. It is the triumph of quiet love, all-comprehending and all-pardoning. The strange woman only loves him for what he can give her. His wife loves him for what she can give to him. Therefore it was decreed from all time that the wife would be victor. Love unspoken is the most tremendous force in the world. One is amazed at the way in which people waste their time making speeches, agitating, praying, even. They might save their breath. The great lovers of the world, in silence, rule the world. Through the glory of their loving the world rushes onwards to God. The only doubt one has is this: Could they, after such a tragedy as had occurred, have found the atmosphere of Far End undisturbed?

Miss Sinclair thinks they could.

'The road went up, bright yellow between its green grass borders. The village was unchanged. The house stood waiting behind its low wall, under its guardian elm, in a golden serenity of beauty. Tall chrysanthemums looked over the wall, the elm was yellowing; but roses still bloomed on the terraces. . . . Far End stood shining and firm, most real among realities.'

It is quite time that somebody compiled a guide-book to that Border-Country.

ONE COMING FROM CALVARY*

WHY does the modern man like to write about the genus old lady? One sees very well why old ladies should like to write about young men, even, with temerity, entering those realms where angels fear to tread—the worlds of sport. Of such was she who wrote 'while all rowed fast, stroke rowed fastest of all.' Young manhood means vitality, joy. It is a law that all things lean outwards, reach upwards to life and light. But why should young manhood occupy itself with those frail, etiolated lives, those denizens of the shut rooms 'facing south,' such as Mr. Sitwell so perfectly describes, furnished with feeding-cups, medicine bottles, and surgical devices; stuffy, often spiritually effete? Is it pity or is it—far more subtle—hatred? Why do so many of those who, in the last war, 'died daily,' write like this? Did they, perhaps, on numb winter mornings with grisly death on either hand and no hope of a to-morrow, think of old ladies sitting by warm fires, knitting? Did they feel an injustice in this, that they must die for these dames who had already enjoyed life for treble their own span, who did nothing, just sitting by fires in their multitudes, waiting to be died for? Not old ladies only; young ladies also, and others, millions of them, all sending their young men to Moloch—their beautiful young men, radiant, bannered with the dawn.

Now, while in Mr. Walpole pity predominates, I think that Mr. Sitwell's book is touched with a kind of unconscious hatred. He is so glad (and so excusably glad!) when Miss Waddington, with her shawls and her 'typically English breakfast,' goes to glory in the bombardment. And all the old ladies in bath chairs 'like giant blackbeetles': the aquarium-like hotel where 'crawl sideways crustacean and armoured spinsters'; the lady with 'as many breasts as Diana of the Ephesians'; the cosmopolitan lady who wishes to find 'a little *ventre-à-terre* in London'—all are etched in vitriol. And that soughing of the tempest afar, presaging, from the steel-grey ocean, the end; how the author revels in it! With what relief could he write of this seaside town as he writes in his fine passage (page 122) about Pompeii— 'Closed for the Winter.' He makes one feel that this carnivorous, drunken, fox-hunting portion of this crowd, hypocritical, secretly obscene, is like the people of Sodom. His considered judgment is icy, terrible. We must remember, when we shiver under this savage irony, that the author and others like him are recently come from Calvary, and that the vinegar they proffer there is surely this vision of life as a bleak irony, a cruel and obscene jest . . .

Of criticism there is little. The redundance on page 300, from page 13, seems unnecessary, and the quotation from Moore is incorrect. It should be 'her *young* hero,' not 'her *dear* hero.' The book is packed with wit, humour and subtlety, and, though liking some of the author's poetry extremely, I had not realised his reserves of intensity until I read his prose.

* 'Before the Bombardment.' By Osbert Sitwell. 7s. 6d. (Duckworth.)

OUR IMMORTAL JANE*

IT MUST be, to most of us, a keen regret that we can never meet Jane Austen, except in a problematical heaven. And what would the angels think of that trenchant wit, that ladylike Falstaffianism? For she had a kind of elfin ribaldry. Would she sit at the Celestial Banquet as she did at the Hampshire tea-parties, with a perfectly solemn face and an infinitely amused mind? There, where the hymn depressingly says, 'no sabbath is o'er,' would she inaugurate with some officiating angel the kind of cat-and-mouse game which she played with Mr. Collins, following his foibles with unescapable keenness and gentle ridicule through the æons of eternity? Humorists are kittle cattle, and Jane Austen is our greatest woman humorist—if not our only one. The Brontës had surprisingly little humour, and George Eliot's was of the obvious rural type. Mrs. Poyser is funny, the Tulliver aunts are quaint, but they do not satisfy; they have not the subtle completeness of Jane Austen's people. What is there about Mr. Collins or Mrs. Allen that we do not know? Mrs. Poyser comes on to the stage and says her say, but Mr. Collins is with us like a familiar friend. It would have been impossible for Charlotte Brontë, who had humour, while Emily seems to have had none, to create Mr. Collins, though she knew the country cleric well. She was too heavily shrouded by the Tragic Muse. What impish things Jane Austen would have done with some of her people! In no sense a poet, she has almost a horror of the deeper

* 'The Novels of Jane Austen.' In 5 volumes. Illustrated. 25s. (Oxford University Press.)

things of life. She is reassuringly mundane. To read her is like turning home in darkness, leaving the planetary systems wheeling on unknown ways, finding fire and candles alight, curtains drawn and supper ready. When we are afraid, after excursions into mystery with the poets, Jane Austen will comfort us. What has Miss Bates to do with death and judgment? Does she want to be in tune with the infinite? She does not. She wants to put on her best gown and go to supper at the Woodhouses'. She wants, if she can circumvent her host, to have a really *good* supper. If everybody kept in this key, how few suicides there would be!

It is one of the most precious things about Jane Austen that she maintains absolute normality and yet is never dull, because, although choosing to remain on the surface, she is an excellent diver. She knows Miss Bates as her Maker does. Many writers of comedies of manners keep to the surface because they cannot dive. They know the outside only of their people, therefore one is bored in a moment. What a pity none of the Miss Bateses in real life knew that they were being so deeply understood! Or did they possibly feel it dimly, blossoming in Jane's human, tonic atmosphere? So by poetic justice she would have her reward, though hidden by the cloudy years from her equals—Meredith and Dickens, Chaucer and Shakespeare, who would no doubt have Bowdlerised his conversation before such a virginal boon-companion. Her rapier wit would have delighted them all, though Dickens's humour is of a different quality, less subtle, less tart, apt, when he allows sentiment to supervene, to be a little mushy, like over-ripe melons. Jane has the stimulus of pickled damsons, which require a certain awareness, while you could eat melon in your sleep.

Though she was lonely—as the great always are—yet she really possessed her chosen souls, who flowered for her, petal by petal, in their shrewdness or inanity, while Jane observed (with pleasure) that Mr. Bennet would never stop teasing his wife until he himself stopped, and (with glee) that if you looked into the furthest recesses of Miss Bates's soul, there was nothing else there at all but the single desire to go to the

Woodhouses' and have as good a meal as might be.

What Miss Austen, beneath her perfectly correct manner, thought of the God Who created so many faces, so many minds, and all with no more in their souls than Miss Bates had, one is afraid to imagine. But if the essence of creative reward is to be appreciated, the Almighty received it in full measure from Jane Austen. Not the finest shade of His tender or cynical humour escaped her, and she was equal to the puzzles He set her. She knew exactly what Lady Bertram would say on a hot summer day: 'It was as much as I could bear. Sitting and calling to Pug, and keeping him from the flower-beds was almost too much for me.' She knows what Mr. Bennet will say when, for the third time in a few weeks, a suitor has come for one of his daughters.

Mr. Bennet, retreating to his library, quite exhausted with the incursions of Eros, remarks,

'If any young men come for Mary or Kitty, send them in, for I am quite at leisure.'

And on another occasion she gets this whimsical gentleman's manner to perfection. He has been teasing his family by refusing to call on Mr. Bingley. Mrs. Bennet is exasperated and scolds the unfortunate Kitty for coughing, because she dare not scold Mr. Bennet. Whereat Mr. Bennet, in his inimitable way, divulges the fact that he *has* called on Mr. Bingley, and adds, as he leaves the room, 'fatigued with the raptures of his wife,'

'*Now*, Kitty, you may cough as much as you chuse.'

And what other writer but Jane Austen would give so sincerely the thought of Elizabeth when her lover returned after she believed him lost to her? Paling, glowing, she yet curbs her mind— demure, shrewd, unconquered.

'Let me first see,' says Elizabeth, 'how he behaves; it will then be early enough for expectation.'

Elizabeth and her father are never just people in a book. They and Mr. Woodhouse were probably Jane's favourite characters, though Mr. Woodhouse should possibly be classed with the more laughable people—Mrs. Norris, Mrs. Allen, Mrs. Jennings and the unsurpassable Miss Bates. Only Mr. Bennet and Elizabeth and a few

more are honoured by serious treatment. To Mr. Bennet she bequeathed one of her own most individual gifts, that of being at once quiet and deadly. No doubt Jane 'suffered fools' in daily life with as imperturbable a manner as Mr. Bennet, of whose behaviour in family squabbles his wife's diatribes give a vivid picture. His ways, his tricks of speech, how familiar they are, like those of a loved father! For Mr. Bennet, for all his irony, is intensely lovable, and is loved by his creator, who revels in shutting him into his study, no doubt with some choice tobacco, away from the vortex of the household. If there is one thing Jane detests more than hypocrisy, it is 'busyness.' She heaps more derision on a fusser like Mrs. Norris than on anyone except a Mr. Collins or a Sir John Middleton, who was 'loud in his praise of every song, and as loud in his conversation while every song lasted'; who also, when asked to describe his friend, could only reiterate, 'He had the nicest little black bitch of a pointer I ever saw.'

Stupidity she cannot tolerate.

'Mary wished to say something very sensible, but knew not how.'

'His talents could not have recommended him at any time.'

'Can he be a sensible man, sir?' asks Elizabeth of her father.

'No, my dear; I think not. I have great hopes of finding him quite the reverse. I am impatient to see him.'

But we have strayed from Mr. Woodhouse, the melancholy hypochondriac, whose daughter 'hoped, by the help of backgammon, to get her father tolerably through the evening.' Mr. Woodhouse's firm conviction is that 'the sooner every party breaks up, the better.' Nobody, after all, thinks Mr. Woodhouse, should take anything but gruel for supper. If they *must*, then let it be 'one of our *small* eggs . . . a *little* bit of tart—a *very* little bit, I do not advise the custard.'

Mr. Woodhouse's dining-room and parlour are among the best of Jane Austen's interiors, in describing and implying which she has few equals. She was not fond of nature. The mute but intense passion of the Brontës for their sombre hills was unknown to her. She regarded picnics as 'parties to eat cold ham and chicken out of doors.' And though she allowed her heroine 'the exquisite enjoyment of air on the summits,' it was only in order that Marianne might sprain her ankle and be carried home with the utmost gentlemanliness by Willoughby. When she says 'it was moonlight, so everybody was full of engagements,' she probably means simply that the roads being what they were, people could only go about in moonlight. She had the circumscribed outlook of her time, and while Turner would have left her cold, a pleasant interior could rouse her to enthusiasm, as in the description of Barton Cottage, of which Mrs. Dashwood's only criticism was: 'I could wish the stairs were handsome.'

In domesticities and social revelries she excels. How she can thrill us when, having got the ideal young gentleman and the perfect young lady into a comfortable drawing-room, she says, 'The instrument was unlocked.'

If she said, 'The mastiff was unchained,' it could not imply more devastating consequences to the young gentleman, for it means that the young lady is going to sing; she might even accompany herself on the harp. Then there were stately revels in the Pump Room, formal calls, complicated dinners of many courses at the ungodly hour of five. These people were un-affectedly interested in their dinner. In a cookery book, published in 1808, are to be seen plans of the various courses at a formal dinner. Each course consisted of twenty-five dishes, and in one course were included pheasant, smelts, collared pork, lampreys, roast hare, 'moonshine pudding,' veal and 'globes of gold web with mottoes in them.'

No doubt Jane knew these mottoes and enjoyed them and the solemnly splendid dishes. This type of life may partly account for the solidarity of her work. She has stamina. Independent, robust, she expresses feminine intuitions with masculine brevity. Her girls are real, for all their primness. So are her men, in spite of their curious clothes. Her d'Arcy and Elizabeth, sparring, are like Beatrice and Benedick. For those finding life terrible, Jane Austen is salvation. Death waits, eternity presses in. We weep and are afraid. Have we not wandered far in the dark night? Have we not lost our loves?

What does she do? She lights the candles and sets out her rich dishes of wit and humour.

'Don't cry!' she says. 'Don't let Emily Brontë sing:

'Cold in the earth, and the deep snow piled above thee.'

'Not *long* living, but *right* living; not death, but the manner of it, are important. Above all, let us be well-bred.'

She herself died with serene courage, and so lived that 'no one could be often in her company without feeling a strong desire for her friendship.' Sweet-voiced, delicate of complexion, slender— she must have been very charming. Perhaps no eight words could express her so well as those on the facsimile title page:

' "SENSE AND SENSIBILITY."
A NOVEL.
BY A LADY.'

The publishers are to be congratulated on the helpful notes, good print and delightful illustrations. The only criticism is that the paper is too good, refusing ingress to its firmly welded pages until after a long struggle with the aching wrist of the eager reader.

LITTLE MISS BURNEY*

To the question, 'Who was Fanny Burney?' quite a large percentage of people to-day would reply that they did not know. Others would say that she was a little authoress who lived at the time of Dr. Johnson and emulated him, writing somewhat stilted letters, in her own person and in the persons of her heroines, in the Johnsonian manner. In her own day the reply would have been, 'She is one of the daughters of that charming Dr. Burney,' or 'Oh, the Blue-stocking of whom the Queen made so much, nobody can imagine why.'

Who and what, then, was this Fanny who managed, without offending the strictest canons of her times, to be a little in advance of them; who could keep, at the routs and gatherings of the wits, her shy demureness, slipping in and out of the conversation like a small, hidling bird, yet able to hold her own; who could spend five years at court and be liked better at the end of it, not for any special wit or skill at her tasks, but for a grave, simple humanity. People told her things about themselves. Mrs. Delany confided how Sir Joseph Banks, the botanist, had praised the ingenuity of her shell flowers. Warren Hastings was cheered at his trial by her quiet sympathy. To her the terrific Doctor Johnson, who had driven the chariot of his ponderous intellect over everybody, sent a message simple as that of a small child—'Tell Fanny to pray for me.' To her Colonel Goldsworthy confessed his misliking for early service at Windsor Chapel in winter, when the King, the parson and himself, 'freeze it out together.' Little Princess Amelia shouts across

* 'The Story of Fanny Burney.' By Muriel Masefield. 6s. net. (Cambridge University Press.)

the drawing-room, 'Miss Burney! Miss Burney! Take me!' And she is frequently surprised playing games with small children. Perhaps the greatest triumph of her sympathy was when the queen, anguished beneath her chill calm by the king's illness, said, 'I thank you, Miss Burney. You have made me cry; it is a great relief to me.' Even more appealing, because of its touch of the grotesque, is the picture of the sick king, breaking away from his doctors and running after Miss Burney and calling upon her name, as one might, frightened by a nightmare. After all, whether we are kings or chimney-sweeps, we are all under threat of a nightmare, and the comfortable people are those after whom we can run when the brooding trees are too heavy and thunder darkens in the sky. Fanny was a comfortable person. That is the most astonishing thing about her. With her satiric gift, her sharp crystal wit, her cumulative paragraphs which have something of the Johnsonian invincibility, her chill, objective style in revealing a character—such as the Captain's in 'Evelina,' with all this, she was yet warm, lovable, helpful, kissable. Here is the surprise of her character—a surprise which all exceptional people give. Fanny's notability came from 'holding the mirror up' not to Nature, but to the fashionable world of her own day, in fact, the smart set. One would have expected that glassiness of exterior containing nothing which is frequently found in the writers on modes. On the contrary, we find her invariably mixing with personalities of strength and integrity, simplicity, *naiveté*.

Mrs. Masefield accents this, but not at all too much. These qualities Fanny's husband had very conspicuously. He was generous and quixotic to a fault. He would rush to uphold any cause—if only it seemed hopeless enough—filling 'a chariot' with weapons of war until it must have rattled like an ironmonger's shop in an earthquake. In between, when Fanny could rest after those long flights in his wake, he gardened with the zeal of simple natures, so that they had 'cabbages every day for one week.' As Fanny wisely remarks—'We had them for too short a time to grow tired of them.' With delighted adoration she watches him sabring the hedge and moving the honeysuckles and lilacs from place to place to their detriment.

Fanny's wit is delicious. When asked by one of those 'literary and ingenious men, animated by a desire to please,' whether she were sorry when he was erroneously announced to be dead, she replied—'Well, sir, as times go, I think when they killed you it is very well they said no harm of you.'

Often she endows even her stupid characters with wit. 'What has he to live upon?' cries young Branghton, 'why, he's a poet, you know, so he may live upon learning.'

Evelina is of course a mistress in wit.

'Mr. Smith called, to acquaint us of the Hampstead Assembly . . . the ball was at the *long room* at Hampstead. This room seems well named, being without ornament, elegance or singularity, merely to be marked by its length. . . . We came home very safe.' To be safe, with Evelina, was to be not a little dull, and was not at all of the quality of the escapades at Vauxhall and Kensington Gardens. But Evelina is far more worldly than Fanny, who, creating her, did not altogether approve of her. Women characters are not her chief claim to genius. It is the Captain Mirvans who give her a right to be mentioned with Fielding. To depict the captain without overstepping the limits of ladylike modesty was indeed a feat wonderfully accomplished.

'The Captain, without inquiring into any particular of the affair, peremptorily declared himself against it.' He roars and tramples through the pages, being 'put in an extacy' by hearing of anybody's misfortune. 'What argufies so many words?' said the Captain, 'It is but a slit of the ear.' He is, to use a country expression, 'the very spit and image' of the worst type of John Bull. Yet in justice we must own that such as he made Nelson's victories possible.

'Odds my life,' cries he to a fop, 'half an hour thinking what you'll put on? I wish I'd been near you! And who the deuce do you think cares the snuff of a candle whether you've anything on or not?' Only a mind of masculine strength allied with a humanity big enough to net the queerest, clumsiest fish, could have produced this inimitable person, and when one thinks that Fanny's chief ambition was to be 'A lady of singular ingenuity and politeness,' it is the more remarkable.

Mrs. Masefield takes a delight in showing us Fanny's picture of herself and her husband at last 'tranquil, undisturbed and undisturbing,' among the roses and jessamine, building 'Camilla Cottage,' 'despairing not of enjoying our dear dwelling.' She loves Fanny, one can see. Her book is as absorbing as a good story, and it reveals beneath its simplicity a store of knowledge of the subject. To reduce so much material to this compass is a difficult feat, here excellently done.

Regretfully finishing this engaging book, one feels that though nowadays authoresses have not Miss Burney's privileges, existing rather in a vast indistinguished herd, like a school of porpoises, we all, at any rate, have our Waterloos. And though Fanny's pleasant intimacy with a king and queen, of manners at once homely and royal, would be difficult in our modern hurly-burly, yet we all, by whatever name we call her, have our Mrs. Schwellenberg, who announces with calm, persistent ferocity, 'I shall do everything that I can to assist you to appear for a nobody.'

IRONY AND MRS. WHARTON*

IRONIC genius is rare, though plenty of us have observed the generous helpings of irony, with or without tragedy, which Fate lades out to us. Nobody, one supposes, ever felt it as the Greeks did—a beautiful race in a lovely summer land, yet obsessed by this dark vision. But after all who is afraid of a dead leaf in winter? Only in the rose gardens of summer is it a threat. So the people of richest vitality and fullest experience are usually those whom irony haunts.

Mrs. Wharton is one of them.

This is what puts a fine point on her drama and gives a steeliness to her work, whether it depicts city or country life. The lover of nature, by the way, must deplore Mrs. Wharton's partiality for writing of cities, because she is so wonderful when she is expressing hills and gardens and the people of the wild who move before the purples and the rich mists of the landscape as emanations of it. Ethan Frome and the people in 'Summer' are of these. Ethan is a marvellously restrained, still, rocky personality. He has, in his setting, a power he would lose in a town, just as the heroine of 'Summer' has a wild-rose charm which would wither if Mrs. Wharton sent her to the city. Hence one finds that whenever Mrs. Wharton deliberately waives her second great gift—the interpretation of nature—her people at once become stereotyped, especially when they are rich people. It is the same with Thomas Hardy, with whom Mrs. Wharton has a decided kinship, for when he leaves the open country we

are always conscious of a dimming of the lustre. So when Mrs. Wharton's millionaires sit around and drink cocktails—amazingly many cocktails! —it is impossible always to remember who said what, and who is who's husband and which of the characters are just bankrupt, divorced or dead. This is not altogether because Mrs. Wharton disapproves of the set she describes, nor because these spoilt children of wealth are necessarily dull, for one cannot help thinking that many rich men must be in their secret souls as wild, fascinating, relentless and ferocious as bandits. It is perhaps because in the hot, scented air of those languorous—often drug-soaked—rooms, where ennui prays for some new thing to prick its failing nerves, where life is one long sluggish dream of 'Twilight Sleep,' she feels that there is something incurably effete, utterly at variance with the storm-beleaguered lives which are her true *métier*.

'Twilight Sleep' is of course a deliberate 'showing-up' of all the absurdities of modern American 'fast' life. That very fact weakens it, for the novelist is not a reformer. If it were not for the sudden exquisite touches of nature, and the solid pathos of Maisie, and the sudden development of Nona in her father's hour of need, one would be almost bored. In chapter after chapter they lounge on divans, ring bells, give orders, go without interest in cars like furnished houses, from places which bore them to other places which bore them rather more. If they would grow a potato, get in their own winter logs, do the household washing—how it would save them! Again, one cannot say, as in that wonderful book, 'The Mother's Recompense,' with its sudden swift-hidden drama silently shattering a life, that the end (the ironic end) crowns all. For somehow the end of 'Twilight Sleep' is less tragic than sordid. One feels that here Mrs. Wharton has plagiarised her own earlier book unconsciously and unsuccessfully.

For whereas there is, in the story of a man who, unknowingly, falls in love with the daughter of his sometime mistress—she and the girl being ignorant of it also—the germ of an almost Œdipus-like tragedy, there is in the adultery of an effete young woman with her father-in-law nothing but a kind of squalor. There is no

* 'Twilight Sleep.' By Edith Wharton. (Appleton.)

inevitability, there is nothing of the sense of helpless humanity struggling in a net set for it before time was. The power of 'A Mother's Recompense' is that we know there is no help for these trapped ones. God Himself cannot let them out.

Still, having achieved such works of genius as this and 'Ethan Frome,' with its astounding ending of the sick wife nursing with life-long devotion her husband and the girl with whom he attempted suicide, and 'The Glimpses of the Moon,' and 'The Age of Innocence,' and 'Summer,' Mrs. Wharton can, without in the least disturbing our allegiance, write what she likes. Only one feels that it is *not* what she likes. And one greatly desires that she will return to the mood and the milieu of 'Summer.'

REVIEW ARTICLES
The Spectator

BIRDS, BEASTS AND TREES

LONG gone are the days when uncles at the Christmas bookshop announced that they 'only' wanted a book for children. Those were the people whose own youth was nourished on 'Cautionary Tales.' With what glee, on solemn festivals of one's own childhood, awed by the authoritative voices of great-great-uncles, did one open the little book with its antique woodcuts, thinking, 'And they believed all this!' After this came the period of self-conscious simplicity, of 'talking-down.' Nowadays the names on Gift Books are among the most distinguished of their time, and there is a predominance of the best of all books for boys and girls—Nature books.

To write a good book of this kind is one of the hardest tasks in the literary world, for to a great store of knowledge must be added a crystal honesty and the power to steep fact in imagination without changing it or twisting it. Also, while such books may be made anthropomorphic to a certain degree, great care must be taken not to humanize the animals too much. It is, perhaps, better not to make them talk, but only to express their imagined thoughts. But if their talk is pure bird-talk and beast-talk it may be all right. The great thing to remember is that Nature is utterly different from, utterly careless of, man, and that there lies its primal fascination.

In reviewing a dozen books dealing with Nature from different angles and in different degrees of intensity it is interesting to trace through them all a connecting idea—the question which seems so slight in itself, but which yet delves to the heart of creation—'Does the animal world, the enormous, bemused, half submerged world of the "not-man," does it think as we think, reason as we reason?'

This question binds together the tersely expressed discovery of science and the simple tale a mother tells her children. Religions have been founded on the diverse answers to the conundrum; thunders have been launched from the thrones of science. But still the creatures of field and forest maintain their reserve; go upon their daily ploys, shy and debonair; weave nests, distil sweets, build cities, dam up tides—and disclose nothing of the inner secret of their accomplishment. The scientist and the child both ask with the same wonder, 'In what furnace was thy brain?'

But while Fabre practically denies reason to animals, the trend of younger thinkers is to allow that they have it, and W. T. Hornaday, in *The Minds and Manners of Wild Animals* (Scribners, 7s. 6d. net), says, quite deliberately, that animals have the same reasoning powers as men. He even goes so far as to assert that they deduce new sets of ideas from old ones; 'think before and after'; model action upon the results of constructive reasoning, and have souls. (This last, of course, means just what the particular religious tenets of the reader allow it to mean. For, to begin with, have we souls ourselves? What and where are they? If the lion and the bee have them, have the jelly fish and the flea also? And to what new domain in the Cosmos will all these souls go after death?) But, apart from this, Mr. Hornaday has built up a sincere and logical argument founded on long and sympathetic study of wild animals. He takes the chief human attributes—courage, obedience, unselfishness—and, having proved animals to possess them, he goes on to show that when these emotions are met by such things as hunger, fear, or imminent death, deliberate reasoning results. He gives instances to show that where the mind of an animal has not been able to fall back upon custom nor the law of the herd, but has had to 'think or die,' it has thought, and thought to good purpose. The Kearton books are also full of such instances. So is one's own observation. But they are also full of opposite instances. The bee, blundering at a partly open window, is not reasoning. It is blindly struggling. It goes foolishly up and down without deducing the fact that the strip of air means liberty. Yet the same bee, confronted by the colossal problem of inventing a new comb-shape (as cited by Tickner Edwards in his *Lore of the Honey Bee*), not only tries to do it, but does it, actually creating a new comb-form. And, the more one watches any creature, the more it seems as if the animal world had access at certain times and not at others to a wisdom deeper than our reason. Perhaps somewhere here lies the germ of the answer to the riddle. The animal world has developed along lines of instinct and intuition which we, in the dim past, discarded for reason, and which we are only just beginning to re-learn. Its failures are not ours, nor its triumphs. On the surface the results of reason and intuition may look the same, but their

intense, their almost awful fascination is that they are not. *We* have been *thinking* hexagons while the bee has been dreaming them. In short, the animal world seems to have access to the mystery behind life, seems to have a 'corner' in the subconscious where man only gropes. May it not be that the animal shows apparent stupidity at one moment and reasoning powers at the next just because under sufficient stress its instinct touches the spring of the subconscious (which includes individual memory, race memory, deductions drawn from them, and something else as yet unnamed) and in a flash it knows its way. So the poet works, in darkness lit by divine flashes; and the poet works by intuition, not reason. May not the animal world be to ours what the poet is to the man of science—a fool maybe, but a fool who is liable at any moment to become a prophet?

Mr. Hornaday's book is the pondered judgment of a practical man on a question of extreme mystery. It is both brilliant and careful, and it is an event in the literature of natural history. If one may make a criticism, it is a pity he did not gather together the threads of his thesis in a final chapter.

Richard Kearton's book, *At Home with Wild Nature* (Cassell, 7s. 6d. net), has the perfection of all his work. He has patience, humour, love and the integrity of the true lover of earth. He never makes a statement without proving it, not once, but many times. Years of comradeship with the peoples of meadow and mountain have enabled him to think the thoughts of the very fledglings a-row upon a brier, and of the tender-crafty mothers in fur and feather. No follower of the Grail could have had a more sincere, indomitable heart than this great observer of small creatures. He follows the flicker of vanishing wings with the ardour of a lover, and no rebuff discourages him. The result is a fairyland of actuality. Few men have taken such intimate pictures of birds as the Keartons. They excel in their photographs of nestlings and mother-birds, and from the expression of the sitters one gathers that the birds are as much at home with them as they are with the birds. Particularly charming is the dipper fronting page 99, which has the essence of 'dipperishness'—the neat, well-tailored air which it never loses even after submersion under rushing water. Some accident of printing has made the blackbird, fronting page 147, look like a thrush; and even Mr. Kearton cannot be allowed to misquote Blake (p. 58) and to call his verse doggerel! But that is one's only criticism of a marvellous book.

The illustrations to W. P. Pycraft's *Birds in Flight* (Gay and Hancock, 15s. net), though they have not the exactitude of the camera, have the delight of colour which so appeals to the mystic and the savage in us all—particularly in children. Mr. Roland Green is to be congratulated on the beauty of these pictures in which he has triumphed over a great difficulty—that of showing the markings on flying birds. In actuality the flying bird is just a blur. It is a pity that in the plates the various birds were not kept to scale, for the wagtail comes out as large as the buzzard. Also, are not the young chaffinches too fully fledged for their size? And is not the bill of the drumming snipe too long? (It is about a quarter of the bird's length in reality.) Most lovely of the pictures is that of the woodcock carrying young. Whether they do really carry them thus, or on the back like a bat, the artist has expressed in this picture the essence of motherly tenderness and baby trust. Apart from such small criticisms one has nothing but unbounded gratitude for such a book, which ought, like Mr. Kearton's, to be on everybody's shelves. The chapters on modes of flight and how to tell birds on the wing are most fascinating— especially to those who know the difficulties of such observation. Whether he describes the dainty love-flight of the grasshopper-warbler or the majestic wing-display of the sun bittern the author is equally happy. This is a book of unique charm, and any schoolroom to which Christmas brings it will become hysterical with delight.

Nature's Curiosity Shop, by Richard Kerr (*Boys' Own Paper*, 6s. net), deals with the freak-ishness and not the homeliness of Nature. It is a valuable addition to Nature lore, and its descriptions and pictures of butterfly eggs, strange caterpillars and birds and 'vegetable sheep' are calculated to rouse in a child's mind the wonder which is one facet of worship.

Romances of the Wild, by H. Mortimer Batten (Blackie and Son, 10s. 6d. net), *Wild Kindred*, by Jean M. Thompson (Jonathan Cape, 6s. net), and *More Nature Stories*, by Waddington Seers (Harrap, 4s. 6d. net), are all well-told stories of wild animals in England and America. They are told from the animal's point of view, which is good, because it awakens boys' imaginations to the feelings of their dumb kindred. But would a fox-cub born in May be able in the autumn to fight a large dog? This occurs in *Romances of the Wild*.

The Pond, by Carl Ewald (Thornton Butter-worth, 6s. net), seems at first sight to be inaccurate, for it seems to confuse the nest, eggs and song of a reed warbler with a bird whose white-barred head shows it to be a sedge warbler. Also, all the colours are too bright and definite for this muted little bird. But the book is translated from the Danish, and there are probably several species of warbler there unknown in England. The humour in the book is subtle, and the entire lack of sentiment is convincing. One may deprecate the manners of Mrs. Spider, who ate her mother and her husband: but one believes in her—alas! Mrs. Reed-Warbler is quite Strindbergian in treatment. It is a charming book by a writer whose works are already classics.

It seems ungracious to criticize *Maya*, by Waldemar Bonsels (Hutchinson, 7s. 6d. net), because there is a real feeling for sensuous beauty in the book and much charm. But men do *not* 'build towers loftier than a queen bee's bridal flight,' nor does the elder blossom in the black-berry season nor winter jessamine in August. And the nurse bee on the first page has not got the worker's pollen baskets nor honey sacks, yet the nurse bee is a worker. And when the beetle asks Maya to have 'some rose honey' surely he is 'pulling her leg,' for the rose is a pollen flower and (one always thought) secretes no honey? But apart from this and from the too-much mixing of fact with fancy, it is an attractive, delightfully illustrated book.

Prince Jan, by Forrestine C. Hooker (Mills and Boon, 6s. net), and *The King of the Snakes*, by Rosetta Baskerville (S.P.C.K., 2s. net), are interesting little books, though too much mixed up with humanity to be, properly speaking, Nature books.

Last (but by no means least) comes *Tommy Smith's Birds*, by Edmund Selous (Methuen, 2s. 6d. net), an unpretentious, but delicious book, written in the redundant, circumstantial manner dear to all simple souls, from a three-year-old to St. John the Divine. The home lives of Mrs. Nuthatch and Mr. and Mrs. Warbler, and the heart-searchings of Mr. Water Ousel at being 'just Mr. Dipper,' will entrance the nursery. This is the book of a large and pleasant personality, and though simple in style it is accurate in matter.

OUR BIRDS, THEIR HAUNTS AND NESTS

THESE are dear little books, just right for small hands to hold. Most of the photographs are beyond praise. They have caught the ancient-wise look of nestlings as well as their delicious downi-ness, roundness and helplessness. Particularly engaging are the young blue-tits and cole-tits and the sternly-fluffy baby kestrels. But the corncrake looks too clumsy in body and too naked of head, and there is something exceedingly wrong with the two examples of swallows' nests. The first is more like a blackbird's nest than anything else, and it is not very much like that. The second might possibly be a swift's nest after it has been leased by starlings and house sparrows. The birds somewhat indecisively labelled 'Crows—Rooks' are not convincing, being too heavily beaked, and the beaks too much curved. They are more like carrion crows. There is also something wrong with the nest in the picture of young chaffinches, though the mother chaffinch on her nest is in every way excellent. One hopes that Messrs. Foulis will soon publish a third and fourth series of these charming books, for though this review may seem to have emphasized the few errors, it has nothing but praise for the books as a whole.

Photographs by Charles Reid. (Foulis. First and Second Series.)

BIRDS, BEASTS AND FLOWERS

Pan's People: the Lure of Little Beasts. By the Hon. Gilbert Coleridge. (T. Fisher Unwin. 9s. net.)

IT IS often the case that the descendant of a great man will become, by a kind of unconscious, inherited sympathy, the exponent and the illustration of one facet of his ancestor's inspiration. And, as the publisher says on the wrapper, the beautiful words from *The Ancient Mariner*, 'He prayeth well who loveth well both man and bird and beast,' very aptly sum up this book by Coleridge's descendant. Mr. Coleridge loves the creatures for themselves, not because they are good sport or good food nor because he owns them. He is one of the few Londoners who know the fascination of Kensington Gardens in the early morning, when, beneath the soft murmur of the tree-tops, companioned by the water-birds, bewitched by the deep voices of the wood-pigeons, one is no more in London, but in some charmed fragment of elfin woodland which has floated up, intact and secret, out of a remote world, whither it will return at the milkman's plaintive cry. The most interesting chapters are those on animal attractions and telepathy. It is a very charming book.

Sidelights on Birds. By H. Knight Horsefield. (Heath Cranton. 12s. 6d. net.)

This book, by the Natural History Editor of the *Yorkshire Weekly Post*, contains some delightful chapters suggesting the possession by birds of occult senses. Anyone who has watched birds must often have wondered if they dipped for their wisdom in the well of subconsciousness. Here is a particularization of this idea. The theory that they, in common with butterflies and other creatures, are subject to magnetism and are able to pick up vibrations, is so strange and lovely that one feels it must be true. One's

criticisms on a book containing so much accurate knowledge are very small ones. Should not 'long-tailed field mouse,' page 35, read 'long-tailed titmouse'? Would not 'twittering' describe the dipper's song better than 'gurgling'? Has any reader seen a cock bullfinch sitting on the eggs, or with a beak like a goldfinch, or with so much black under his chin, as in the picture facing page 88? The present writer has not. Apart from these trifles this is an enchanting book.

Round the Year in Richmond Park. By H. R. Hall. (Selwyn and Blount. 2s. net.)

This book must be bought by all Londoners, who will be surprised to see how rich they are in trees, birds and plants. The reader is told what is to be seen month by month, and where to look for it. There are also complete lists, giving English and botanical names, and a map. It is interesting to see what a number of real country wild-flowers, such as ling, heartsease, comfrey and forget-me-not, grow practically in London. A delightful book, in which the illustrations by H. B. Whanslaw are a very attractive feature.

Green Timber Trails. By William G. Chapman. (Parsons. 8s. 6d. net.)

Although the author of these stories of wild life is a hunter, they are written, at least partially, from the wild creature's point of view, and will therefore do good and not harm to boys' imaginations. They are full of thrilling accounts of the Canadian forest and its furry inhabitants by one who (though paradoxically) loves them.

The Deeside Field. Edited by A. Macdonald and J. B. Philip. (The Rosemount Press.)

These collected addresses of the Deeside Club are full of interesting facts. Field clubs are excellent things, not only because they provide accurate local knowledge, but because they give an excuse for people of all ages to set aside their work and their troubles for a time and become boys and girls again.

Pamphlets of the Whins School of Herb Growing.
By Mrs. M. Grieve, F.R.H.S. (The Whins School,
Chalfont St. Peter.)

Theory and practice are united, it seems, at the
Whins. The reviving of such private enterprise as
this for the growing, gathering and drying of
medicinal herbs is a splendid idea. Not only is
instruction given as to growing culinary and
medical herbs, but a market is offered to individual collectors of wild plants which would otherwise be wasted. The special pamphlets on various
plants are full of interesting things—quotations
from old herbals, modern recipes, derivations of
names, quotations from the poets, and the names
of the diseases for which the plants are good.
Those interested in this fascinating subject
should write to Chalfont St. Peter for some of the
pamphlets.

WILD LIFE IN MANY LANDS*

O VERSEAS Nature books are fascinating (and
difficult) to review, because of the strange-
ness of their fauna and flora. Turning their pages,
finding only a few familiar creatures in a host of
strangers, is like waking on one's second morning
in Eden, having fitted a few of the flowers and
beasts with names on the previous day, but with
most of the wild denizens of Paradise still
unhanselled by their taming and endearing
epithets.

Western Birds,[1] by an American woman, bears
the authentic imprint of the impassioned lover
of earth. This love of earth is oftener found in
men than in women, perhaps because it is only
recently that woman has ceased to be a pampered
being, who dared not go out in the rain. Harriet
Myers knows the thrill—the real, heart-stirring
thrill—of seeing for the first time a rare bird or
a new sub-species of plant. She has also the
unquestioning patience without which nobody can
enter the charmed country, and a humour which
responds to the quiet glee with which the furred
and feathered people always seem to look on life.
Her book, so far as one who has never been to
America can judge, gives a full, exact and valuable,

* (1) *Western Birds.* By Harriet Williams Myers,
London: Macmillan. (18s. net.)—(2) *A Natural-
ist's Holiday by the Sea.* By Arthur de Carle
Sowerby, F.R.G.S., F.Z.S., M.B.O.U. London:
Routledge. (7s. 6d. net.)—(3) *A Perthshire
Naturalist.* By Henry Coates, F.S.A.Scot. London:
Fisher Unwin. (18s. net.)—(4) *The Text-Book of
Pomology.* By J. H. Gourley, M.S. The
Macmillan Co., New York. (12s. net.)—(5) *Mate-
ship with Birds.* By A. H. Chisholm. Melbourne:
Whitcombe. (7s. 6d. net.)—(6) *Allotment Garden-
ing for Profit.* By E. T. Ellis, F.R.H.S. London:
Clarke. (2s. net.)

as well as a very interesting, account of the birds of Western America. She is a keen and precise observer, and her descriptions are so careful in detail that even a beginner could hardly fail to recognize the birds on sight. Many naturalists fail in this. They forget that what is familiar to them is not so to everybody. Nothing is more difficult than to recognize the various species of birds in one genus. Take the willow-wrens. Even when they are still it needs more than a casual glance to distinguish some of them—the reed and sedge warblers, for instance. And in their native haunts, flitting bee-like in the shadowy, sun-flecked cavern of some huge tree, or slipping through the brookside undergrowth, it is not easy, even with the help of good glasses and after years of watching, to name them. It is in this that a book like *Western Birds*, with its nicety and vividness, is of such help.

Mrs. Myers says rather wistfully that she has never heard a water-ousel sing. She has a delicious treat in store. Nothing but a naiad ever made music so wild and so crystalline and of such a liquid sweetness. There is one small criticism to make. The paragraph beginning 'The common call of the adult flicker' occurs in two places, pages 37 and 40. Probably the author did not see her English proofs.

A Naturalist's Holiday by the Sea[2] is full of happiness, knowledge and ozone. Mr. Sowerby and his son evidently had 'the time of their lives' in Cornwall, and the book allows the reader to share in their pleasure and to learn a great many new and interesting facts. The chapters about eels and submerged forests are especially fascinating. The story of the eel has been well known for some years, thanks to the Scandinavian researchers, but it always bears retelling. The gist of it is this. The eel, that lives its mute and bounded life in some stirless pond, lost and forgotten as a grave, with no higher aim than the day's food and the night's rest, keeps, all the while, a blazing vision in her soul. Of that she dreams; for that she prepares, changing from dull ugliness to silver beauty. The dream grows stronger. The pond cannot hold her. She is for the sea—the vast, the terrible, the beautiful. There comes a dark, rainy night when she is

gone from the pond, lashing across the wet meadows to the nearest running water, and so to the sea. She has begun her epic journey. Reckless, she flings herself over the huge shelf out at sea, where the unplumbed deeps of the ocean begin. Sleepless, fasting, she takes her undeviating course, until she reaches the radiant blue abysses off the West Indies. And the motive? What could the motive be for such a journey but love—desire—the need of beauty for beauty, the necessity for creation, for young? And the end of this marvellous travelling, the fit and divine end, is death. There is no return from this mating in the profound mystery of the sea. Only the young return, slipping back by hereditary instinct to the quiet pools, to prepare for their own heroic life-story. Space does not allow mention of the submerged forests, rocks and shells and water-birds on which the author discourses so delightfully, but everybody who is going to the sea for the holidays ought to take this book.

A Perthshire Naturalist[3] is the exquisitely simple, homely life-story of a postman naturalist. And those few who do not already know what delightful people country postmen are will learn it from this book. There is a quietude about them, a philosophy that comes of their day-long communing with hill and forest and wide skies. There is courage, for in the wild winter the mountain postman's round is often full of real danger. And there is sympathy, for he is the confidant of everybody on his round, and he hears, as he leans on the garden gate beneath the arch of yew or roses, while Granny Somebody opens her letter with trembling hands, how Jimmy has got a rise, or Selina has bettered herself, or Matilda has been 'shouted in church.' He thinks of all these life stories on his lonely trampings. He is, as it were, their Providence. His heart is heavy when there is in his wallet a black-edged letter. He will wait a long while at the gate of an evening so that Jane may have time to find the only envelope in the house for her letter to her sweetheart 'at America.' All these qualities Charles Macintosh had, with the addition of a genius for the understanding of Nature. There could be no better life for a naturalist than that of a walking postman in such a countryside. And

Charles Macintosh made the most excellent use of his opportunities, gathering through a long life much valuable first-hand knowledge about the birds and plants, the geology and antiquities of his native hills. And surely in a world which has grown almost meaningless with noise, this peaceful chronicle of a useful and gentle life, with its faithful work and its 'outings' to play at merrymakings, its sympathy, honesty and kindness, is of more value than many sermons.

The Text-Book of Pomology[4] belongs to the Rural Text-Book Series, and contains a very full and exact account of modern American methods of orchard planting and management. It contains many interesting diagrams and plates, and also many statistics which will be all the more attractive to the professional gardener because they are too scientific for the mere amateur. It is obviously impossible for an English reviewer to do full justice to such a book, for the American orchard differs from the English one, not only in scale, but in soil and climate, and therefore in the methods used, and even in the species of tree. The account of experiments in various orchards, and their results, and the discussion of modern methods will, however, be of the greatest interest to gardeners all the world over.

Mateship with Birds,[5] a book about the birds of Australia, by an ornithologist who is also an editor, is a pleasant, breezy affair and will make delightful reading for boys and girls. Its only fault is that it is too much of a mixture. It is not solid natural history, nor is it quite to be classed as journalism, nor could it possibly be called *belles-lettres.* This gives the reader a sense of unrest. This is a pity, because the author has a deep love for the things of which he writes, and his ideas and point of view are always likeable. If Mr. Chisholm crystallized his style and chastened it he would write excellent Nature essays, which could really be classed as *belles-lettres.*

Allotment Gardening for Profit[6] will probably be very useful to the townsman for whom it is primarily intended, though it contains little that a country dweller would not know. But in gardening, as in everything else, it is a question of 'If to do were as easy as to know what were good to do . . .' and therefore Mr. Ellis's insistence on common sense in small details will be of real use. It is so dreadfully easy *not* to thin out one's turnips sufficiently. It is so sadly difficult to grow a broccoli of the perfect beauty possessed by the illustration. The broccoli of amateurs is apt to be stringy in leaf, yellow in flower, and less like a close, generous bouquet than like antlers with sparse blossom at the end. The value of Mr. Ellis's book is that he not only says that such marvels of perfection can be grown by anybody, but he even insists with fury that they *must* be grown by everybody. Many a gardener will put down the book with a blush and hasten guiltily to his overcrowded seed beds. And one is sure that nothing could give the author greater satisfaction.

SENSE AND SENSIBILITY OUT OF DOORS*

ONE can gauge a character by its attitude to Nature. From the imaginative to the starkly realistic is a far cry, yet there are true lovers of earth in both camps. Each of us, wandering in a wood, creates it, and these woods that we make are as diverse and as many as the flowers in a hedgerow. To the hunter the wood is a place of tracks and spoors, faint footmarks, secret dens—the place that conceals or reveals his quarry. So Mr. McConnochie regards it.[1] In his fascinating account of the Scotch forests, with their sweet-sounding names and their ancient mystery, one is always conscious that the primary absorption of the author is sport, and that on the next page something will probably be killed. Still, shooting is the most merciful of sports, and deer-stalking is a brave antique craft, and has nothing in common with the ignoble and cruel pursuits so often called sport. To the ordinary reader the book will be interesting. To the sportsman it will be absorbing.

To the scientist a wood is the abode of the especial fungus, flower or fly on which his mind is concentrated. Fabre had that point of view, and Major Hingston[2] reminds one of that great naturalist. He has the same clarity of mind, exactitude, curiosity, inexhaustible patience and complete lack of sentiment. He watches the amusing spectacle of an ant industriously 'milking' a greenfly without being tempted to deduce any moral therefrom, or to think that either party is actuated by altruism. He wonders what causes the phenomenon, and he proceeds, by a series of minute and practical experiments, to find out. His account of the byre-building ants and burying beetles has, like all his work, the magic of sheer, hard-won truth.

To the author of *One Garden*[3] a wood is compact of wonder; of friendly voices calling, friendly faces peering; of leafy marvels that can be taken home to the beloved garden. The author is 'the very marrow' of a gardener, and is able, as some of the best practical gardeners are not, to express the dewy passion for roots and buds. This pleasant book is a mixture of sense and sensibility. There was, perhaps, too little sensibility in our first two books. There is certainly too much in *The Glory of the Garden*.[4] It is a pity that such a likeable little book should be marred by this sentimental attitude. It is as unwise to be sentimental towards Nature as it would be to sonnetize in her presence the rosy lips of a cannibal queen.

* (1) *The Deer and Deer Forests of Scotland.* By A. Inkson McConnochie, F.Z.S. London: Witherby. (25s. net.)—(2) *A Naturalist in Hindustan.* By Major R. W. G. Hingston, M.C., M.B., I.M.S. London: Witherby. (16s. net.)—(3) *One Garden.* By D. H. Moutray Read. London: Williams and Norgate. (12s. 6d. net.)—(4) *The Glory of the Garden.* By M. G. Kennedy-Bell, F.R.H.S. London: Black. (5s. net.)

'WHEN THE PIE WAS OPENED'*

* (1) *Birds and Their Young.* By T. A. Coward, M.Sc., &c. Illustrated by Roland Green, F.Z.S. London: Gay and Hancock. (10s. 6d. net.)— (2) *The Wonder Book of Nature.* Edited by Harry Golding, F.R.G.S. Illustrated. London: Ward, Lock. (6s. net.)—(3) *British Birds.* By Percival Westell, F.L.S. Illustrated by Doris Meyer. The Abbey Nature Books. London: Chapman and Dodd. (5s. net.)—(4) *British Butterflies and Moths.* Same author and publisher. (3s. 6d. net.)— (5) *British Insects.* Same author, publisher and price.—(6) *British Reptiles, Amphibians and Fresh-Water Fishes.* Same author, publisher and price. (7) *By Meadow, Grove and Stream.* By Henry Hilton Brown, F.E.S. Illustrated. London: R.T.S. (3s. net.)—(8) *Dragons and Dragon Slayers.* By Frederick W. Hackwood. Illustrated by Gordon Browne, R.I. Same publisher and price.—(9) *Skewbald, The New Forest Pony.* By Allen W. Seaby. Illustrated. London: Black. (5s. net.)—(10) *Barbrooke Grubb, Pathfinder.* By N. J. Davidson, B.A. Illustrated. London: Seeley, Service. (3s. 6d. net.)—(11) *The Adventures of Twinkley Eyes.* By Allen Chaffee. Illustrated. London: Grant Richards. (5s. net.)—(12) *Tiny Toilers and Their Works.* By G. Glenwood Clark. Illustrated. London: Harrap. (3s. 6d. net.)

WHEN the parcel of review books came, the birds did indeed begin to sing. Before, one had just been a dull grown-up person in a room in London, wondering if the sun was going to get through the fog. Came Carter Paterson, Santa Claus of daily life, with twelve Nature books for children, and the sun *did* come out. Not only that. Also, the London sky folded itself up neatly, selvedge to selvedge, and put itself away in a drawer with the grown-up feeling and winter. A vast blue heaven, where larks hung like Christmas-tree angels, arched above, and a small child wandered in the standing hay-grass of a long-suffering father. Forests of ox-eye daisies and quaker-grass waved above the white clover and the red. Butterflies stood on their heads in ecstasy. Bumble-bees rushed by with the crescendo and diminuendo sound of tiny express trains. Mysterious walls of fragrance rose about one— pink above the clover, white where the hawthorn was, blue at the entrance to the hyacinth wood— thick, soft walls through which you could walk to more marvels. And, as I said, the birds began to sing, 'All at once, and all in tune.' Piping and fluting, whistling and trilling, while the grave, recollected blackbird uttered his mastering melody and the cuckoo's two notes throbbed like a pulse, they made the place all in a charm. 'They cherme as byrds do when they make a noyse a great nomber together.' Starlings, reckless with joy, mimicked the predatory owl, hooting with clownish glee. The insect world was no whit behind. The crickets laid on to their fiddles very heartily, like a Covent Garden orchestra in Tannhauser. No creature but had its note of gaiety. No tree but had its nest. No plant lacked its flower or bud. And when dusk came, and the sweet smell of dew, still the feast and the song went on. Over the mauve ladysmocks thrilled the grasshopper-warbler. Moths gyrated solemnly to amuse their mates, or put on masks (as the puss-moth does) to alarm unwelcome guests. The night-jar's spinning-wheel had been busy a long while when—hark! it is the father's bed-time call. Through long shadows and moony gleams the child runs home, secure in the faith that 'to-morrow will be as to-day, and much more abundant.'

Aware of the enormity of such disquisitions, I return to my parcel. If blame is due for the vision, let it be borne by those wizards, Mr. Roland Green, Mr. Pycraft and the other authors and artists mentioned below.

Last year I had the pleasure of reviewing Mr. Pycraft's *Birds in Flight*, illustrated by Mr. Green. This year the same artist has collaborated with Mr. Coward, whose book, *Bird Haunts and Nature Memories*, was one of the interesting collections of Nature essays last year, though it had not the charm of the present volume, *Birds and their Young*.[1] Youngness is the essence of this book, and in the depicting of youngness Mr. Green is an adept. Delightful are the baby shell-ducks with their expression of derring-do, and the long-tailed tits seated before their elaborate domicile. The dipper and her domed nest are good also, though the artist has forgotten her white eyelashes. This brings me to my chief criticism. The other-wise perfect picture on the wrapper is marred by the fact that the hen robin is painted as bright in breast as the cock. I have never seen one more than faintly red, the main colour being a sort of yellowy brown. The hen yellow-hammer also seems to me too bright. Is feminism spreading to the avian world? The hawks are very well done, with the innocent-relentless look that all birds of prey have. The tinting is delicate and rich, especially in the painting of woodcock. There is an amusing drawing of a tern offering, in a nonchalant manner, a fish to his lady. In his very able chapters Mr. Coward begins with the nest and takes us full-circle through infancy, helpless or precocious adolescence, food and feeding grounds, lessons in flight, bird language and maturity, to the courtship display. He tells us not only of the mating music, but of the drum-ming of snipe, the roding of woodcock, the linnet exhibiting his rosy breast, the lap-wing placing

bits of grass before his chosen partner, and whirling round in an offhand manner as if to say, 'A nest? My idea! Take it or leave it.' This is a book of great merit, and so is *The Wonder Book of Nature*,[2] to which Mr. Pycraft and other distinguished naturalists have contributed. Mr. Golding is an excellent editor, and has arranged such a repast of mingled wonder and beauty as will delight all children. From African lions to a rose-leaf cut by a bee, from Vesuvius to a diatom, the subjects range, illustrated by scientific plates and by pictures of woodland glades and daffodils and branches of blossom. There are some coloured plates too, and Mr. Roland Green appears again as a painter of butterflies. In the diverse chapters we hear, among other things, what the flowers are doing at night, what the trees are doing in winter, how butterflies make them-selves look like leaves, and insects turn themselves into musical instruments. Mr. Charles Whymper's painting of an eagle, with its frame of soft gold, makes a beautiful cover design. 'The Abbey Nature Books'[3,4,5,6] are a mine of information about almost all forms of animate life in the British Isles (the book on mammals was published previously). The salient facts about each species are tersely and clearly expressed, and the author manages to include in small space most of the things we want to know. Many books of this kind are disappointing because they so often leave out the very thing one is looking for. Mr. Westell has not only a vast store of knowl-edge, writing as easily about fish and lizards, frogs, dragonflies, and beetles as he does about birds and butterflies but he has the gift of im-parting it in concentrated form. This is just what is wanted in popular Nature books. In the bird book he gives an index of families with the various birds belonging to each. In the volume itself each bird has about a page. The other volumes are on the same lines, and those on insects and reptiles are unusually interesting, because these are comparatively seldom treated of. The illustrations by Doris Meyer are very good, especially the coloured ones in the bird book. The dipper on page 80 is unconvincing. Though there is nothing absolutely wrong with it, the artist has not caught the likeness. Also, on the wrapper of *Butterflies and Moths*, the Painted Lady seems, in colour, too much like a tortoiseshell.

I must mention, risking the accusation of a 'robin complex,' that Mr. Westell holds the same theory about hen robins as Mr. Green. Now, either these two authorities are wrong, or all the dear, dowdy little hen robins I have ever met have been frauds or freaks, which would seem to make Nature herself wrong. What is the way out of this dilemma?

By Meadow, Grove and Stream[7] is a pleasant book of leafy gossip including chapters on familiar butterflies, birds, flowers and trees, illustrated with drawings. The silverweed is referred to as goosegrass, a name I thought belonged exclusively to one of the bedstraws. Three boys' books come next. *Dragons and Dragon Slayers*[8] is not a Nature book except by virtue of the last chapter, which treats of dinosaurs and other real dragons; but it must be included because of Gordon Browne's lovely illustrations, which will fascinate boys. *Skewbald, The New Forest Pony*[9] has some good descriptions of moorland and forest, their fauna and flora, wild weather, and ponies galloping across purple table-lands or going in Indian file along green rides. *Barbrooke Grubb*[10] in spite of its dreadful title, has some good chapters about egg collecting and Chaco wizards. *The Adventures of Twinkley Eyes*[11] is a book of charming stories for tiny children. There are no nightmares in it, for none of the furry folk are ever killed. Last comes a very unusual book. *Tiny Toilers*[12] ought to be in every schoolroom. It tells of ants that make gardens and mushroom-beds, keep cows, grow rice, and sew leaves together by using their own live babies as needles. This sounds like a fairy tale, but it is scientifically correct. The magic of it is making me once more feel as if the London sky were folding itself away. Therefore I must cease.

NATURAL HISTORY

IN HIS beautiful book, *Game Birds and Wild-Fowl of Great Britain and Ireland*, Mr. Thorburn not only holds the mirror up to Nature, giving us the perfect presentment, perfect in line and colour and poise, of grouse, mallard, wigeon, partridge and the rest—that alone would earn our gratitude, and he has done it—but has also achieved what comparatively few painters of birds do achieve. He has given us not merely birds, but *Bird*, the very essence and innermost soul of Bird—the creature that dwells behind that soft array of tinted feathers, beyond that arch gaze, haunting the horizons of being as migratory birds haunt the horizons of the world. And, speaking of horizons, we come on one of the secrets of Mr. Thorburn's success. For not only does he create delicious landscapes for his birds, but these landscapes—except in the case of such water-birds as frequent the close, high banks of streams—all have distant horizons. There is the gentle arable country for the partridge, rolling away to low, tree-crowned hills, blue with distance; purple vistas of mountain beyond mountain, with rifts and inlets of the Highland seas, for the kingly black grouse; far wintry skies, and misty shoals, and cliffs that hang like coloured cloud beyond the water, for teal and wigeon and grey lag-goose. And this is right. For, while the near landscape is man's, and the middle distance belongs to the company of timid furred people that rove the woods and meadows, the horizon, ever fugitive, is the heritage of the adventurous wing. Perhaps the most fascinating of all are the pictures of black grouse

Game Birds and Wild-Fowl. By A. Thorburn. (Longmans. £5 5s. net.)

on the wing, and of red grouse in heather. But there are some enchanting water pictures also. The book is so large that the thirty plates are of the size of an ordinary small water-colour. The author also gives a short description of the haunts and habits of the birds depicted. An ideal book for a Christmas present.

The Forests of India. By E. P. Stebbing. Vol. II. (John Lane. £2 2s. net.)

We reviewed at length the first volume of Professor Stebbing's important and authoritative work on the forests of India. We cannot do more than call attention to this second volume and say that the high standard of the first has been maintained. Professor Stebbing tells us that, contrary to his original hope, a third volume will be necessary. The greater part of the second volume is devoted to the period 1865 to 1870. The experiences that have been gained in India are invaluable to foresters all over the world. If we have a criticism to offer it is not of Professor Stebbing's work, but of the manner in which timber is shaped and transported in India. Labour-saving devices are few and far between. Of course, labour is cheap and abundant in India. That is the explanation, though we are not sure that it is economically a justification.

Children—of every age—who like original ideas will be charmed with Miss Curtis Brown's collection of 'Quite Wild Animals.' The drawings, which are reminiscent of Lear's delightful figures, are very convincing, while the character sketches of the mythical beasts are most entertaining reading. The only test of a Christmas book is to try it on a child and the present writer has tried this on two children, who were so delighted with its contents that they insisted on choosing one animal each which was to be their own. The first choice, with which, of course, the elder child 'got away', was the beautiful 'Doolyboo'—a sweet and lady-like animal with a naive glance and a flexible neck something like a giraffe's. So attractive is this animal that the author breaks into verse in the description. The younger child had to put up with 'Blumpleby,' who, it may be surmised, would be a more entertaining companion than the 'Doolyboo.' Whether she was attracted by the fact that the 'Blumpleby' has not had a bath for 3 years, 8 months and 4 days, I do not know, but though his habits as described in the text are unpleasant, there is a twinkle in the eye of his portrait which says much for his talents as boon companion. The book can be recommended as a charming Christmas present for any child with a whimsical sense of humour.

Quite Wild Animals by Beatrice Curtis Brown (Heinemann)

THE HONEY BEE

From Virgil, via Huber, to Tickner Edwards —through that immense tract of time with its rather sparse bee-literature—one may have travelled in spirit, exploring the withheld secrets of this fascinating creature. Yet, confronted for the first time in any practical capacity by the real thing, by bees perturbed, enquiring, enraged; by bee-music rising from a deep murmur to a furious uproar; by obstinate, inexplicit brown masses that insist upon going where you do not want them to go, and obdurately refuse to enter the hive so beautifully prepared—does one remember a single word that one has read? Few creatures so tiny have managed to raise such unreasoning panic, and though in the born bee master or mistress this panic will almost immediately change to a kind of joyful recklessness, it is unpleasant while it lasts. Both to those suffering from it and to those who have achieved success Mr. Mace's book will be welcome, for he is not only a born bee-master with a great store of practical knowledge, but he does not mind chronicling his difficulties and early mistakes. These being everybody's difficulties, the exact account of Mr. Mace's way of escape from them, his hasty expedient at a crisis, will help a beginner far more than libraries of careful theories. For dealings with

Adventures Among Bees. By Herbert Mace. (Hutchinson. 4s. 6d. net.)

bees, almost more than with any other living thing, are really a series of unexpected crises. When the author tells of the broken section on the floor of the hive most bee-keepers will remember the same thing, and worse, happening in their experience, and will wish they had been as competent. This is only a small thing, but it can cause dreadful disorder in a hive. As for his swarming adventures—but let the reader see for himself. Of all the inventions of the bee, swarming is the one which can least be met by theories. It is a case of picking up a skep and putting your best foot foremost. Those legends of elvish leadings of poor mortals over bush, over briar, might well have arisen out of the adventures of bee-keepers at swarming time.

Mr. Mace's deductions as to the best kinds of bees to keep, the best way to avoid or combat Isle of Wight disease, and the simplest methods of driving the bees are most valuable. Speaking of breeds, there is a breed of bees still extant in the hills of Shropshire which is called about there the Old English Bee, and which is smaller, fiercer and (I think) darker in colour than the ordinary hive bee. It is very hardy, and can face a mountain winter in the thinnest of boxes. It would be interesting to know whether readers have met this bee in other parts of the country, and whether bee-keepers think it superior or inferior to Mr. Mace's favourite Dutch bee.

The chapter on honey secretion in flowers is fascinating. The author says that hive bees can get honey out of red clover, which is popularly supposed to be only a bumble-bee flower, in a second or poor crop, because the flowers are more stunted and the corolla therefore shorter. He also noticed that in a field of white clover under constant observation only some birds'-foot trefoil was visited by the honey bees, and not the white clover, that most popular of bee flowers. Could this possibly have been due to the fact that some other clover-loving insect had visited it in large numbers? This is only a guess, but it might explain what is otherwise a conundrum.

This delightful book is illustrated by the author, and bee-keepers will do well to buy it and his other work, *A Book About the Bee*, also published by Hutchinson.

DABBLING IN THE DEW

The Wonder Book of Plant Life. By Henri Fabre. Translated by Bernard Miall. Illustrated. (T. Fisher Unwin. 15s. net.)

The Spirit of the Wild. By H. W. Shepheard-Walwyn. Illustrated. (Bodley Head. 12s. 6d. net.)

Prints from Many Trails. By H. M. Batten. Illustrated. (Herbert Jenkins. 12s. 6d. net.)

Sanctuaries for Birds. H. J. Massingham. Illustrated. (Bell. 5s. net.)

How to Enjoy the Countryside. Marcus Woodward. (Hodder and Stoughton. 2s. 6d. net.)

By Shank and by Crank. By Edmund Vale. Illustrated. (Blackwood. 15s. net.)

Impressions of Great Naturalists. By Henry Fairfield Osborn. (Scribner's Sons. 12s. 6d.)

'IT's dabbling in the dew that makes the milk-maids fair,' says the ballad. And it's dabbling in the dew that makes the naturalist a success. No matter how much he knows; how sweetly he 'speaks with the tongues of men and of angels,' he will never make a naturalist unless he dabbles. One has come across work which was perfect, and yet was ruined by some tiny slip, revealing the non-dabbler. For though the brain of an Aristotle and the style of a Pater were united, they could not win a smile from the brotherhood of earth, unless their possessor could also show a dewy chrism.

All these six nature books, though very different in scope, have this in common—their authors dabble in the dew. The seventh is a book about nature lovers of the more purely scientific type, who dabble not only in dew, but in the life-blood of earth. Comrade of these is the first author on my list—Henri Fabre. This marvellous genius shows himself in quite a new aspect in this book —*The Wonder Book of Plant Life*. Except for various individual and unmistakable Fabre passages, one might almost think it had been written by a son, inspired with his father's knowledge and steeped in his spiritual atmosphere. Fabre is, as it were, on holiday. That almost painful concentration and relentlessness of observation is not called into play as it is in the insect books. He has wandered into the world of green and golden mystery, where the secret is forever almost (but never quite) revealed, where we seek our Host, that we may thank Him for what Fabre so beautifully calls 'a frail magnificence.' For a time his benignant face is bent over the gentler doings of the plant world—factories of gum and resin and aromatic oils. He is here primarily the observer, full of wonder. In his own special province he is not only the observer. He sees, but he must look beneath what he sees. He is not the artist, gazing on a lovely head. He is the surgeon with a scalpel. That is why in this book, where he allows himself to gaze and wonder, we see a new Fabre—a Fabre who, instead of lingering with sorrowful but stern truthfulness on the fierce minds of insects—and no tiger could be fiercer than some of these— tells us of the delicious stickiness of buds and sweetness of leaves 'when the spring is in travail.'

The book is an account of the plant, beginning before the plant existed, telling of the sleep of plants, the movements of leaves, the unity between the form of the cotyledon and the structure of the stem (a fascinating and almost unexplored subject, this union between the forms of various parts of a plant, as in the passion flower, where the pollen-grain, a round box with a lid, is almost exactly like the centre of the flower in shape); of the flow of sap and the amazing mysteries of fertilization; of the bud which, he says, 'is the plant'; of trees so ancient that they seem like gods, and trees so young that they look out, trepidant, from their kindly seed-case; and (of course) of the relations of the insect world with the plant world. And he also tells us why these things are, and how they come to pass. Perhaps the most remarkable sentence in the book is that in which he says that he believes plants to have 'a shadowy vestige of the instinct existing in animals.' That is not too wonderful for Fabre to believe. He is, in fact, one of the apostles of wonder among scientific men.

Mr. Shepheard-Walwyn has a pleasantly con-spiratorial way of saying, 'This is his path!' or 'She always comes this way!' as if the badger's or the squirrel's coming were a royal progress. And so it is, of beauty and innocence. The most charming description is that of the author finding a sleeping dormouse underground, breathing 'like a broken-winded horse,' and of how he held it in his hand and found its fur *cold*. A study-window writer would have said a great deal about the *warm* ball of fur. Mr. Shepheard-Walwyn says exactly what he saw, and the plainer the writing the more rapture his memories bring to the reader. Only the true naturalist dares

to be terse and simple. The other is nervous as to the quality of his material, and he embroiders. For this reason one would prefer the chapter-headings to be just 'Craft,' 'Mercury,' &c., and not 'The Spirit of Craft,' because it is not of the spirit of this or that, but of otters tobogganing and badgers making their beds that we want the author to tell us in this delightful book, inspired entirely by personal observation. The illustrations are by well-known naturalists, including Kearton, and are first-rate, like those in Mr. Mortimer Batten's short stories. These are as good as the rest of his work—which means *very* good. He has an artless way of throwing on the blank sheet of one's spiritual vision a sudden enormous picture in colour. His settings of black rock and stag-moss, cloudberries, deer walking with gentle *hauteur* from hill to hill, all like a carving seen against a brilliant sky, make us catch our breath. In these stories, the author has come up against the difficulty which all nature-lovers must realize —the antithesis between the naturalist and the sportsman. So, in 'Kreet's Great Lover,' his own friend shoots the bird he has loved all summer, and in the story about the peregrines the sports-man hopes he has aimed badly! You cannot serve two masters in this, though the author evades the difficulty very well in 'Pilgrims of the Sna' Brew.' The touch of the psychic in the book is, I think, a pity. It detracts from the convincing-ness, and we can get plenty of people to tell us ghost stories, but nobody except Mr. Batten can tell us his own absolutely real nature stories, of which we can never have too many. This is also true of Mr. Massingham's writings about birds, which are practical in aspect but poetical in idea. How Darwin would have loved these bird-sanctuaries where, Mr. Massingham says, 'as one walks down the silent grassy aisles, the buttony eyes of sitting birds stare out at one from every angle.' What a perfect little picture it is! Everyone who cares for birds ought to read this book, which is full of magic, so that one has only to open it to hear twittering and flutterings and to see the preening of soft breasts. And whoever reads it will certainly want to go and make a sanctuary immediately. The splendid buzzard, the delicious linnet, and the guillemots, looking like gentlemen at an archidiaconal conference, have all had their photographs taken for the book. There are only two queries. The author says, 'wrens like to swing about' (in their nests). What wrens? Not the ordinary wren, surely? He also speaks of 'grey-limbed alders.' But alders are black, or, at least, all those I have seen are, and it is one of their spring surprises to clothe that blackness in the most delicate of greens. The title of Mr. Woodward's book is both too didactic and too moderate for a nature book. Nature is either nothing to us, or intolerably lovely. But this he could not avoid, for the book is one of a series.

Mr. Woodward sometimes has the gift of magic, but his style is unequal. For instance, it is first-rate to describe the brimstone butterfly as 'a primrose that has taken wings,' but it spoils the primrose idea when he has the word seven times on one page (44). And his use of 'urgent' is good, but when he has it a second time on page 24 its force is dissipated. The book is a series of essays about all kinds of country delights—sheep-shearing, rambles, old field-names, pleasant customs, and the sharp, sweet joy of grass and trees, rain, April and high summer. But where, oh, where, do they wear smock-frocks still in England? If Mr. Woodward knows, let him in mercy say! Only a few times in babyhood did I ever see a smock frock worn by 'an old ancient man,' whose sons laughed at him for wearing it. Mr. Vale's essays also bring before one scenes of country life, but it is not only English country life, and one of the best is a description of how he journeyed in Japan to a far-off volcanic mountain. The spirit of adventure is in the book, and the joy of attained horizons. The first essay describes a walk from Herefordshire into Wales across a bit of Shropshire which is one of the unspoilt and lovely stretches of hill and valley still existing in England. Walking and cycling are the best of all ways of seeing the country, and Mr. Vale knows it, and also knows how to inspire his reader with his own enthusiasm. It is a sure sign of merit in a book of this kind when one wants to go and do likewise. The last book is valuable in a very different way from any of the others. It gives character sketches of scientists from the point of view of one of them. But though Mr. Osborn has many scientific books to his credit, and has written this one from that angle, it seems to have been popular, judging by the frequent reprints. And it deserves to be popular, both for its letterpress and its portraits. Darwin, Huxley, Roosevelt and Cope are some of the great men included, and I am sure all those naturalists now writing would be glad to think that they would find a biographer as brilliant, perceptive and sympathetic as Mr. Osborn.

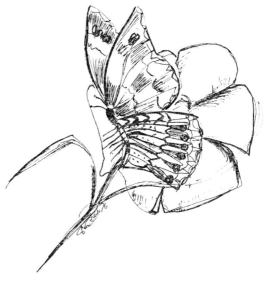

THE WAYFARING TREE

(1) *Nature Studies of a Boy Naturalist.* By C. T. Astley Maberley. Illustrated. (Fisher Unwin. 9s.)

(2) *A Practical Guide to Nature Study.* By J. H. Crabtree, F.R.P.S. Illustrated. (Jarrolds. 7s. 6d. net.)

(3) *Plants and Man.* F. O. Bower, Sc.D., LL.D., F.R.S. Illustrated. (Macmillan. 14s. net.)

(4) *Round About the Sussex Downs.* By Frederick Wood. Illustrated. (Duckworth. 7s. 6d. net.)

(5) *Moorland Mysteries.* By J. K. Bateson. Illustrated. (Herbert Jenkins. 10s. 6d. net.)

(6) *The Old Houses of Stratford-upon-Avon.* By H. E. Forrest, F.L.S. Illustrated. (Methuen. 7s. 6d. and £1 1s.)

WHAT a tree it is—the wayfaring tree! Not the wild guelder rose, which has been honoured by this charming name because it sets its round creamy-white bosses of flowers along many hedge-rows, where grows also the 'travellers' joy.' Not that tree, but the mystic tree which, like those of ancient fame, under whose boughs an army, horse and man, could rest, spreads its arms wide as the sky. It is rooted in the land beyond the horizon. Its branches, rosed with dawn and raddled with night, spread afar over Africa, to the lost lands of the snows, to China, to the seas in the South. They lace the round world with magical shadows, and finger the steep, dark mountains. If you have heard the sound of the Wayfaring Tree, harping like a great cedar, you will have a hunger for the beyond; you will want to put your hat on your head and your shoes on your feet and slip out of the house in the dawn and go by foot or horse or ship wherever its song leads you. It is this tree that the bees hear when they swarm. It is this that lures the caravan across the desert and all migratory birds and beasts to other places—to the new places, the adventurous and sweet places. It is a freemasonry as huge as the world, this freemasonry of the Wayfaring Tree. Very few have failed to share in it, from the top-heavy toddler who has to be deterred from lonely exploration by a board across the door, to the veteran whose life has been full of zest and adventure and who greets death with the joyous curiosity of a bird launching itself across the sea. In that mood the only place that can hold us is the *other* place; the only book that can charm us is a book with distance in it. And as, in June, all the world is filled with the 'desire of distances,' the books mentioned here should be popular. I choose first *Nature Studies of a Boy Naturalist* (1) because of its youthful *élan*, its sincerity and simplicity, its spontaneous manner, and its beautiful pen-and-ink drawings. It is very remarkable that anyone so young should not only have acquired such a great deal of knowledge from personal observation, but should be able to write of it with ease and without the didactic touch from which the very young writer usually suffers. That he can also draw from the wild model itself, and get his pictures like life, is a thing which marks him as one of the very gifted people. His pictures of the hawk and falcon tribe and of fawns are especially good. His opening sentence, too, is instinct with the real spirit of the wild. How this book would have delighted Jefferies and Hudson! And what a pleasure it is to see, by the preface, that it has delighted at least one great living naturalist— Edward Step. In *A Practical Guide to Nature Study* (2) the far country is the one which lies within and beyond our own meadow, spinney or pond. The author says: 'Where should he go to find the lapwing, the long-tailed tit, the dipper or the oyster-catcher?' In which sentence he proves himself a member of our freemasonry. He knows, too, where the grey snake is at home, and how to take a portrait of the green-cup moss. His style is plain, and he is mainly concerned with the practical aspect of things. He can tell you the dental formula of a univalve; press a wild flower so that it keeps its colour; or bottle a tadpole. The plates are clear and good and help us towards what the author well describes as 'a unique view of Nature's secrets.' This interesting book deals with Nature apart from man. Mr. Bower's book (3) deals with it in conjunction with man. The world's plants and their uses to humanity is a big subject, and one which Mr. Bower handles with brilliant success. From the humble potato to the splendid cactus; from Kentish pine-woods to bamboo groves in Ceylon, his illustrations range, and there is one of lovely seaplants under the water. The scope of the book, the immense stores of its knowledge, the brilliance and clearness of its style, recall Fabre. From the leaf he works up to the plant-body generally, to woods, fields, gardens, orchards, fungi, bacteria,

ending with two excellent chapters on man's dependence and influence on vegetation.

Mr. Bower is already well known as one of our distinguished botanists, and this book will certainly add much to his fame. *Round About the Sussex Downs* (4) has not only a picture of black oxen at work, but of a dewpond! The delight of these is also in the letterpress, except when it treats of the horrid lore of 'sport.' But this part of the book can be regarded as negligible, and you can then share the author's real and happily expressed pleasure in the downs and the blue sky, small birds, trees, untrodden ways and the tribes of the flowers. Some of these, by the way, mentioned in the author's calendar, seem to have been found at surprising dates. January 1st is so early for Shepherd's Purse, and April 28th so late for Mercury. But Sussex probably arranges its floral clock differently from Shropshire. There is a charming description of 'going to the hill' on page 189; the author is especially happy in this vein, and we should all, I am sure, like more of it—a book full of these delights and free of the trail of sport. In *Moorland Mysteries* (5) we go to wilder scenes. The manner of their treatment is reminiscent of Miss Mitford or of the present-day books of Lady Catherine Gaskell. Human stories are woven into the landscape in a leisurely, naive manner, with humour and a sense of pathos. One likes to think of the authoress and her man safe after the horrors of the War, living their happy life on the little Devonian farm. Incidentally, the writer reveals a charming personality— that of a woman who really knows how to be a man's 'help-meet,' and who is so wrapped up in this self-chosen career (and what a magnificent career, given the man to fit the part of 'Boss'!) that she has no time to think of herself at all. My last book (6) deals with human habitations and not with the outdoor world; but, as it is an account of a wayfaring to Shakespeare's town by one who has a great knowledge of and reverence for ancient and beautiful things, it is in place here. You can hear how Roger Paget was Master of the Guild long and long ago, and how 'the Sisteren' give twopence a year for the cherishing of brotherly love, and were, further, obliged to pay a fine of one halfpenny if they quarrelled 'after the bell has sounded!' And many other pleasant things you may hear to bring a tear or a smile or to fire the imagination. For facts, tenderly treated, are as good a food for the soul as for the mind, and Mr. Forrest is well fitted to gather from them (to use his own words) 'the glamour of mystery and romance which time alone imparts,' for he has not only enthusiasm but also he really knows his subject.

Reviews of Novels of Country Life

The Runaway by M. E. Francis (Hutchinson)

The novels of Mrs. Francis have so secure a place in our country fiction that it seems impertinent to blame and almost invidious to praise. Therefore it is with timidity that the reviewer takes exception to the hero of the tale. It is not that he runs away from his wife. That is excusable. It is not that he tires of being a laird and becomes a blacksmith. That is laudable. It is not because he makes love (in a serpentless Eden) to a yellow-haired young woman. That is only to be expected. It is that twice (once might have been pardoned, but twice!) he, who has been brought up in the country, does, while lifting potatoes, *throw down his fork*. He damns himself. He is confessed a fool. Our sympathies turn to his shrewish wife. No wonder the grandfather of the golden-haired young woman laughs in his beard (which sounds unhygienic), for did anybody, since Adam delved and Eve span, ever hear of a gardener who threw down his fork? Is it not the immemorial custom, when a real gardener goes to his lunch, to jab the spade or fork very scientifically into the earth in a perpendicular position and for the handle to be immediately tenanted by a robin?

The Forge In The Forest by Charles D. G. Roberts (Dent)

The Forge In The Forest is a thrilling story— thrilling in the manner of Stevenson, with whom the author has a decided kinship, though his work is entirely individual. He is already well known as the writer of delightful nature books, and in this book also, though it is not primarily about nature, one immediately notices the sure touch of a lover of earth who not only loves, but knows. Mr. Roberts belongs to that gracious company which includes writers so various as Thoreau, Stevenson, Hudson, Mrs. Gaskell, Miss Mitford and Mary Wilkins. The reader is the willing bondsman of these charming people. He does not mind what they write about, so long as they will write. It may be only letters, or it may be a story like *Catriona*. If there is in it the delicate emanation of the writer's soul, all is well. Mr. Roberts has, in this book, achieved a style which is at once vivid, limpid and strong.

After Harvest by Charles Fielding Marsh (Allen & Unwin)

Mr. Marsh is an author who deserves commendation, if only for his industry and his honourable ambition. In conception and treatment, 'After Harvest' is distinctly above the average, but it is uninspired and uninspiring, a rural novel in which the expected always happens. It concerns Priscilla Postle, a town-bred young woman who lends herself, though with considerable reluctance, to a plan whereby John Thirtle, a farmer of dissolute habits, is to be won from his evil courses. This plan, conceived by his widowed mother, is simply that he shall marry a virtuous girl who, by precept and example, will keep his mind on higher things, namely, herself and the welfare of the farm. Mr. Marsh is admirably clear-sighted in his view of his heroine, whom a less intelligent or less conscientious writer would have glossed over with the varnish of sentiment. Priscilla Postle's passion for self-sacrifice is born, as her author recognises, of certain priggishness or spiritual pride. The characterization of Mrs. Thirtle and of son John, is equally penetrating, but Reuben, John's half brother, is a somewhat insubstantial figure. The story moves forward at the leisurely pace we have learned to expect of such stories; and, though it suffers in our esteem by reason of its fidelity to a dull formula, it has enough of sober merit to have been worth writing.

Off The High Road by Annette Reid

These are short stories of English country life, told with great charm and simplicity. They are practically all stories of frustration, and though the writer prefers to stay on the surface of her characters, and not to pierce very deeply into the 'heart with blood red-tinctured', yet so far as they go they are true to life. It is life as seen by the innocent daughter of a country vicar or doctor, not as seen by a Tolstoy or a Hardy, yet it is real life. 'Martha's Treasure' is excellent, and the last story is quite perfect. Its tragedy is the eternal one of mistaken, interfering kindness. The woman in it simply wants her freedom, her cottage and the management of her own life. High-handed people arrange that she is to be looked after, to live with somebody else, away from her own home, to attain prosperity—and misery. Mr. Brock's lovely little pictures give grace to the stories and the book as a whole is fragrant with country content and redolent of peace. It is also charmingly produced.

La Bodega (*The Fruit of the Vine*). By Vicente Blasco Ibanez. (Fisher Unwin. 7s. 6d. net.)

There is in the work of Ibanez a large humanity which probably explains his popularity. For one usually finds that whether a popular book is a work of genius (the public does occasionally patronize genius) or a work of no artistic value, it has this quality of human charity. Ibanez stands between these extremes. His work is very good, but, at any rate when read in translation, it is not genius. But in its gift of sympathy for all sorts and conditions of men, though possibly in nothing else, it is kin to that of Dickens. Listen to this (necessarily shortened) dream of the rustic bride-to-be:

> 'They would arise at break of day, . . . she to prepare breakfast and tidy the house. He would mount his horse. Not a button would be missing in his jacket, his shirt would always be as white as snow, as well ironed as any owned by a Jerez gentleman. And when he would return she would be at the gate waiting for him, with flowers in her hair and an apron so white that it would blind him. The stew would perfume the whole house. They would sleep in the holy tranquillity of those who make good use of their day, and do not feel the remorse of having wronged anyone.'

Very homely and naïve, may be, but it is exactly what a country girl would think. It is true to life as are the descriptions of the poor people who keep cattle and horses in the Spanish hills, of the vine-dressers and the rest of the agricultural population. One may never have been to Spain, yet one knows that they are true to life, for beneath the surface humanity is the same in nearly all parts of the world. And though in writing of grand folk Ibanez is often superficial, he does manage to get very near to the peasant heart.

The Red Redmaynes by Eden Phillpots

Why is it that, when Mr. Eden Phillpots grows tired of unalleviated Dartmoor and brings in a detective story to heighten the interest one feels as if he had momentarily doffed the purple? What is the origin of one's obstinate conviction that a detective story is not literature? Probably it is because from the moment when the detective comes in, the author's preoccupation, like the detective's in real life, is with the mere actions of the criminal, and hardly at all with the fears, hopes or agonies that drove him to crime. This makes one inclined to call even the finest detective story literary journalism, not creative literature. There is *Hamlet* of course. At least in part it is a detective story, with Hamlet as private detective. But he is occupied with his mother's soul not with the particular brand of poison used. His methods are exactly the opposite of a detective's, being intuitive. The real detective story is intellectual, not intuitive. Great art is intuitive. This is why we feel that Mr. Phillpots, in writing this kind of book instead of the type in which he simply interprets moor and mountain, and the people who dwell in them and express them, has taken a step down. As a detective story this is a brilliant piece of work. It hangs together well. It is logical, technically perfect and very thrilling. The only thing that is wrong is the initial premise. For no young couple with ordinary instincts, civilised, even humanitarian, as these two were, could possibly engage in such cold blooded crime, unless they were mad. And they cannot both have been mad. In fact, the author depicts them both early in the book as being eminently sane. None the less this is an enthralling story.

*   *   *   *

The Path to the Sun. By Netta Syrett. (Hutchinson. 7s. 6d. net.)

Miss Syrett's books always have charm. This has an ultra-modern theme, which is rather refreshing. It expresses the reaction from such things as psycho-analysis, aestheticism, consciously educational homes and a certain type of modern school. Her idea at the beginning seems to be that because Tristram and Caia are brought up thus they are failures, and because Priscilla escapes she is a success. Afterwards, however, Miss Syrett implies that Priscilla is a success because she is vital, and that she is vital because she is the love-child of a vividly alive woman, while the others are the legitimate children of a dull woman, by the same father. Anyway, Priscilla is delightful.

Streets of Night. By John Dos Passos. (Martin Secker. 7s. 6d. net.)

Fundamentally this story is a psychological study of the relations between children and parents, or rather, of the effect of parents upon children. Superficially it concerns the emotional inter-relations of three young Americans in Boston, two men and a girl. Just as in abstract design the unfilled spaces are as important to the whole as the filled portions, if not more important, so with this story; the things which Mr. Dos Passos has not said explicitly, but which he has left to the knowledge and insight of the reader, are by far the most significant. He has set down the effects and inferred the causes. In this respect he has drunk deeply of the Russians. Incidentally, it is a method of subtle flattery to the reader, and so increases his good opinion as well as his appreciation of the author. This makes it none the less a legitimate and effective method, and it has been employed here with skill. In other respects, too, this book is an improvement on Mr. Dos Passos' earlier work, in spite of the melodramatic title. He has gained a finer control of his medium. His economy is exquisite. But he is still a little consciously literary and portentously serious. There is not one spark of humour in the whole book. His failure to understand and explain the girl as thoroughly and clearly as the men produces a slight dissatisfaction with the characterization. But it is nevertheless a good book and worth reading.

POEMS

GLADYS MEREDITH. c. 21 years.

THE MESSENGER

As a pale moth passes
In the April grasses,
So I come and go
Softlier than snow.
Swifter than a star
Through the heart I flee,
Singing things that are
And things that cannot be.
I whisper to the mole,
And the cold fish in the sea,
And to man's wistful soul
Life sendeth me.
As a grey moth passes
Through October grasses
So I come and go,
Softlier than snow.

EARLY POEMS, circa 1898-1907

SPRING   *1898*

*Earliest extant poem, written at The Woodlands,
Stanton-upon-Hine-Heath, when she was seventeen.*

Come out beneath the hoary apple trees!
Their boughs are rich with myriad shades of green,
Blushing with flowers
Which throw sweet petals on the balmy breeze
Down to the grass, which seems to nod and lean
Under their showers.

The tufted grass is hardly seen for flowers—
Cowslips, and daisies tall, with yellow eyes,
And bluebells fair,
While high above the rest the hemlock towers,
And clover (courted by the butterflies)
Perfumes the air.

Now suddenly there breaks upon the ear
The bleating of the sheep upon that hill—
With sunlight fair;
And then (so low that we can scarcely hear)
Comes from more distant fields the answer, till
It fills the air.

And all the time the drowsy hum of bees
Comes o'er the clover like a lullaby,
Telling of rest,
Joined to the cuckoo's call from the larchen trees
That wave their feathery branches up on high
With fircones drest.

Now blends the sound of a far distant bell
(Floating along upon the western breeze)
Chiming the hour.
And the lark's song, which we all love so well,
Comes thrilling down among the budding trees
With sweetest power.

The laughter of some children gathering flowers
Rings sweet and merry from beside the stream
Where thrushes sing.
Sweet sights and sounds amid the falling showers,
The scent of blossom mixed as in a dream—
This is the Spring.

THE GATES OF GOLD AND GREEN*   *1902*

Nature has opened her gates again!
Her gates of gold and green;
Has opened them wide to welcome me
Back to her glorious liberty,
To her wholesome grass and sun and rain,
Through her gates of gold and green.

The infinite sky bends close to me
With a great protecting calm,
And wave upon wave of its peace profound
Steals on my spirit and circles me round
With the stillness of eternity
And a great protecting calm.

   * *Written during convalescence when recovering
from her first serious illness.*

THE FAWN (Pastel)

Hark! In the willows mute
A sedge-bird tunes his flute.
In the lean, leafless spindle
Rose-points kindle.
The pines, one by one,
Bow down to the sun.
And God comes to me down the lawn
In the guise of a fawn.

SHEPHERD'S SONG

March on, dark shadows! up the mountain side,
And quench the flaming of the blood-red heather.
Come like an army or an ocean tide,
Till not the eastern hills and valleys only,
But all the western slopes are merged together,
Even to the peaks, in darkness vague and lonely.

Ascend the sky, grey clouds! and pall the moon,
So it may be a night without a star.
Let earth and heaven be merged; then soon, ah, soon!
All else obliterated, I shall see
Away along the valley, shining far,
Her yellow lamp, my star of destiny.

DAWN

One lonely bird,
Singing his heart away,
Just before dawn—
Four on a Summer's day,
Earth drowned in sleep,
Pale cloudless sky:
Watch for the sun we keep—
Blackbird and I.

Just that one song
Floods all the place;
Brims over earth,
Floats into Space.
Silvery notes come first,
Thrilling with love;
Then in one glorious burst—
'Praise God above!'

June 1902

THE WHITE MOTH

Over the fields at the fall of dusk,
Glamour is far and near.
Grasshopper-warblers are whispering
Close in the ear.

Delicate lavender ladysmocks
Shimmer along the way;
Eerie and wan in the afterglow
They bend and sway.

Down by the stream in the deepening night
Magical odours creep,
Breath of basil and mallow and musk
Falling asleep.

Under the moon, when the world is hushed,
If you were there to see,
Wonderful things are happening
In the willow-tree.

The furry white moth has a cradle there,
Hid in the silver bark.
She wakens and stirs at the rise of the moon,
And wings through the dark.

The sweet white campion is calling here
With fragrant voice in the night:
Deep in the heart of that glimmering cup
She tastes delight.

I worship the earth and the airs that blow!
Churches and Creeds are nothing to me,
I have my church where the daisies grow,
Under a whispering sycamore tree.
For God is deep in the sycamore's heart;
He is in the eagle that seeks its prey;
He is up where the flashing meteors dart;
At the hills' deep roots—in the open day.

He is in the storm as it sweeps along;
In the murmuring stream, and the song of a bee;
In the hymn of right—in the so-called wrong,
He that created them, there is He.
So God being over, and under, and in,
Filling the world as His joy fills me,
Can there dwell with Him temptation or sin?
No. There is nought but to love and to be.

So I do not fast, nor grieve, nor pray;
But dwell in the beautiful, blest and free,
Breathing God's loveliness every day,
Living my life in an ecstasy.
When the shadows of sunrise lie
Right across the awaking earth,
When the earliest bee drones by,
I sing aloud with ecstatic mirth!

When the shadows are sweetly green,
Where reflections of wild rose faces
Sleep in the brook, I will plunge, unseen,
Save by rats from their secret places.
I'll race the ripples of meadow-grass,
Overtaken by shadows of cloud,
Watching the wheeling plovers pass,
Hearing them plaintively calling aloud.

And every night I shall reach the hills
That lay in the dawn so far and blue;
Where peace flows down with the flowing rills,
And every magical thing seems true.
And so to sleep on the topmost hill,
Under the moon with the world afar;
I shall not stir while the dews distill,
Till morning quenches the morning star.

FRAGMENT

Into a broken heart
Wandered a magic word.
Straightway it woke and heard
Nature's low laughter.
Henceforth it dwelt possessed
With a divine unrest—
While the slow music came,
While the song rose like a flame,
Burning so bright and clear . . .

There are the pastures of sleep
And creatures at rest;
A mountain enchanted and steep
Floats on the west.

And there, like a blossoming tree
On a dew-drenched lawn,
My playmate is waiting for me
In the luminous dawn.

THE SEDGE-WARBLER

Among the green rushes he wakens and sings
Alone in the dusky hush—
Long, long ere the blackbird has shaken his wings
And piped to the slumbering thrush.

Then labourers, treading the earliest dew,
Rejoice in the delicate strain,
And eyes that have waked the weary night through
Can smile on the morning again.

To listeners impatient of silence and night
The brave little tender lay
Gives sweeter surprise and a deeper delight
Than all the great chorus of day.

The long iteration of noonday doves—
The raptures of blackbird and lark—
For the children of joy! But the sorrowful loves
The minstrel who pierces the dark!

THE HERITAGE

Dull? . . . When the full moon slips in silver past my window-pane,
Just as she slipped by the porphyry arch and shone on Sappho dreaming;
And winds that howled round Nineveh's walls and brought old Babylon rain
Come, like ravens with wide black wings, to waken me with their screaming?

Sad? . . . When my saffron crocus holds a brown bee in its cup,
Just as on Hybla's purple hill, where the honey was warm and yellow;
And every day in my quiet room the crystal light stands up
Pure and sweet as on Olivet when the autumn days grew mellow?

THUNDERBOLTS*

Stretched at harvesters' ease we lay,
Burnt nigh black, where the poppies thickened,
Never a thing had we to say,
Thunder rolled in the hills all day.

My shirt was torn and I reeked of sweat;
All my body was blazing and quickened.
She was untidy and sulky, yet
Something about her you couldn't forget.

I got my knife and began to hack
Elder whistles to keep me quiet.
'Jim', she said, as she lay there slack,
'I won't go on, and we can't go back.'

I asked what she meant, but I knew. The sight
Of her scornful look made my blood go riot,
I showed her a poppy, straight and bright,
Crushed in my hand: we stilled at the sight.

Thunder broke on the hills at night.

* Scarlet poppies are called thunderbolts in
Shropshire.

CATERINA TO CAMOENS*

O Luiz, Luiz! In those early days
You little thought what bitter tears would flow
When you knelt down and laid your first fresh bays
Before my feet, and kneeling watched me go.
And when you crowned me with your noble praise,
And breathed—'My Lady!'—reverently and low,
You never dreamed how lonely were my ways
For your —'My Love!'—which I might never know,
Because the dust—such golden dust to me—
Was thick about you, in a place apart
With weary rest you circled in my heart,
And haloed me with immortality.
But (Mother of grief and love, forgive me this!)
I would have given all for Camoens' kiss.

* Camoens, the Portuguese poet.

POEMS TO HER FATHER 1909-10

(George E. Meredith died 5th January, 1909)

THE LITTLE SORROW*

Within my heart a little sorrow crept
    And wept and wept.
Below the lilt of happiest melodies
    I heard its sighs
And cried: You little alien in my heart,
    Depart. Depart!

When suddenly a shadow crossed the floor
    And through the door
The Tragic Herald passed
    And blew a blast
Which drowned all music and made loud the air
    With wild despair.

Amid the harsh, discordant sounds of fate
    I listening wait:
Not hoping that a song can reach my ear;
    But just to hear
The little weeping grief I once bade cease
    Would now be peace.

* *Full version of the poem. The middle verse is not included in* Poems And The Spring Of Joy *(Cape, 1928), p. 85.*

UNFINISHED EMBROIDERY

On that last night, embroidering by his bed,
I often paused, his loving smile to meet,
And hear the tender approving words he said:—
'Your work is very beautiful, my sweet!'

The embroidery stays unfinished; Life's design
Must yet be stitched. How can I raise my head—
And no smile there? Lest sudden tears of mine
Should stain the cloth, and dull the silver thread.

For when the work is spread before his eyes
It must not seem too sadly incomplete.
So he may smile and say in glad surprise,
'Your work is very beautiful, my sweet.'

1909

THE FOOTPATH (I) To G.E.M.

The path his daily footsteps made
Across our field dies not away.
We could not bear to see it fade,
And so we walk there every day.
And when we reach the further gate,
We almost see him standing there
In just the way he used to wait,
With sunlight on his silver hair.

His life was like a pathway, straight
And lovely, over peaceful ways
Right on beyond the sunset gate;
We long to tread it all our days.
And maybe, when we reach the end,
The old, sweet smile will light his eyes,
And round his silver hair will bend
The aureole lights of other skies.

THE FOOTPATH (II) (Loss)

The foot-path that he trod each day
Among the changing grass is gone.
So the beloved may steal away,
        And we live on!

The shining thought, the stable deed—
I did not think that they could pass,
Yet they are lost in bitter weed
        And sodden grass.

Beloved! Beloved! I hear in the darkness
Without my close casement, a sound as of fingers.
Oh, is it thy spirit that pleads for an entrance
While near the old homestead it wistfully lingers?
I open the pane. It is raining and raining,
There is nothing out there but the river's complaining.

Beloved! I wake in the cold hour of midnight,
And all round the house goes a desolate sighing,
So homeless and sad that my heart is near breaking
To think it my dear one, so wearily crying.
I lean out and wait, but the night does not hold thee
And only the wind's wild arms clasp and enfold me.

RONDEAU REDOUBLÉ

(To my Father)

I hear your voice along the wind,
You whisper through the melting skies,
The deeps of dawn recall your mind,
The steady stars reflect your eyes.

If, in some far-off Paradise,
With powerful peace you slept entwined,
How could I cry with glad surprise—
I hear your voice along the wind?

Whene'er in sorrow unresigned,
I ask:—'Sends *Love* such agonies?'
'The Lord of Life is wondrous kind'—
You whisper through the melting skies.

When all the hope within me dies,
Your light around my dark I find;
From you to me a message flies,
The deeps of dawn recall your mind.

And when with tears of sorrow blind,
I cannot sever truth from lies,
You come in dreams, my way's assigned,
The steady stars reflect your eyes.

Ah! mystery of mysteries!
Like some fair moonbeam thrice refined,
From God to me your presence lies,
Once, Now, Forever, are combined—
I hear your voice.

1909

THE WONDROUS VOICE

How haunting was the dream that came to you
Three nights before Death brought the interpretation!—
A dream in which you quivered through and through
With one great minstrel's resonant iteration.

You heard a strange, sweet voice, that sang and sang
Within a vaulted chamber—low and dim
And vaguely shadowy; and the shadows rang
With the continual beauty of the hymn.

You thought the music came from overhead
From some high gallery whence it rose and fell:
But who the singer was, and what he said,
Although you longed to know, you could not tell.

A little chill of awe within the voice
Flowed like a river through a summer pleasance;
You shivered, yet you could not but rejoice,
So great and gracious seemed the unknown presence.

Each note—severely tender as the snow—
Built up a song eternal, as a swallow's
Achieving silver heights, or murmuring low,
While evermore another stanza follows.

And all the while your hungry heart was longing
To know the meaning of the song you heard,
Wherein you felt mysterious echoes thronging,
And infinite joy within each hidden word.

You know it now. Ah yes! You know full well,
As in your low and quiet house you lie,
Forever cradled in the golden swell
Of that Great Voice of Immortality.

January 1910

QUICK SWALLOWS

Quick swallows, cosmopolitans of the air,
Come often to their nests beneath the eaves.
Free winds that haunt infinity—vast and bare—
Descend at dawn, and walk among the leaves.
The monarch of the zenith brings his light
To earth at evening, like a homing lark.
And stars upon the topmost towers of night
Oft fling their silver beauty down the dark.
All these inhabitants of aloof, high spaces,
Stoop sometimes to a humbler destiny;
Yet you come never from your royal places
To my low life, to cheer and solace me.
Dear love, come down the stairways of the past,
Consolingly to speak with me at last!

One to whom life was pain, and death a charnel-house, came under cloudy hollows stained with sunrise into a country pleasant as lilac in the rain. Wandering down aisles of birdsong to the brink of a river, she drank where the ousels and the stars had been before her, and found comfort and joy. So she brought back in the palm of her hand for those in need of healing a few drops of the water which sparkled and held the sky.

1910*

* *Mary's Introduction to the First Edition of the* Spring of Joy *(Dent, 1917), omitted in the post-humous edition of the Collected Works.*

[*Calendar Sequence—date approx. 1912*]

January

Hark how the first thrush sends his arrowy music—
Golden and clear—across the driving snow-storm!
See how the violet alder-buds are folded
         On sleeping summer!

Flashes a blue wing in the sombre pine-tree,
Burns a red berry over the bleak hedgerow;
Through the cold snow Life's opal buds are mustering—
         Frail, yet immortal.

February

Now the black yews are set with yellow blossoms,
And the pale winter-heliotrope beneath them
Sends through the frost a delicate, wild fragrance,
         Like a June hayfield.

Who set those red buds on the wych-elm branches?
Who made a rosary of the silver sallow?
Would I might know the Painter of the primrose!
         'Follow and find Me.'

March

Lengthening shadows deepen into purple;
Freshly the bright grass quickens in the meadows;
Clear green and lucent are the elm-samaras,
         Soft as the day-break.

From the low swamp-moss, budding into ivory;
From dark blue valleys prophesying April;
From the red West, that flushes with a secret,
         Some-one has called us.

April

Into wild fragrance break a thousand orchards,
Vocal, mysterious with their deep bee-music.
Stooping, I gather up a single petal
    Blown by the dawn-breeze.

Fragile its scent, elusive as a shadow—
Like a frail bridge flung wide across a chasm.
It is my bridge. I cross, and reach the highway
    To the Eternal.

May

High on the hills, beneath a leaning hawthorn,
Trickles a spring, and one white flower comes sailing
Leisurely, while I watch it journeying seaward
    With its reflection.

In the strange beauty of the curving petals—
Hearted with dim rose-purple—in the marvel
Of the flower-spirit lies my mystic pathway
    To Him who called me.

June

From the green dawn to the green eve I waited
Down in the meadows of pale purple blossoms,
Watching to see the grey moth in the willow
    Break her wan cerement.

Straight—when her wonder grew a little stiller—
She closed her wings above the honied campion.
So I pass on to the high feast of beauty—
    Her fellow-pilgrim.

AMONG THE HILLS

Here dawn slips up in a glory,
And twilight falls in a dream;
And life is a wonderful story
Discoursed by the stream.

The air is a Rood-screen holy,
And the song of the hills cannot cease;
For the fingers of God linger slowly
O'er the key-board of peace.

POEMS AND FRAGMENTS, circa 1914-18

TO MY DEAR

I give you laughing names, dear, for I see
Tears like a sea stand up before the sun,
And the whole world grown dark with tragedy,
And life cut off before the laugh is done.

The plovers are shrill to-night,
For the moon is urgent with them, and silence presses
Close on their brains, on their round wings molten-white
That cleave through light into further wildernesses of light.

AUTUMN, 1914*

The scarlet-jewelled ashtree sighed—'He cometh,
For whom no wine is poured and no bee hummeth.'

The huddled bean-sheaves under the moon,
Like black tents, will be vanished soon.
So fast the days draw in and are over,
So early the bees are gone from the clover—
Today, tomorrow—
And nights are dark, and as cold as sorrow.

He's gone, her man, so good with his hands
In the harvest field and the lambing shed.
Straight ran his share in the deep ploughlands—
And now he marches among the dead.

The ash let fall her gems, and moaned—'He cometh,
And no bee hummeth.'

'O children, come in from your soldier-play
In the black bean tents! The night is falling;
Owls with their shuddering cry are calling;
A dog howls, lonely, far away.'

His son comes in like a ghost through the door.
He'll be ready, maybe, for the next big war.

O world, come in from the leasowes grey
And cold, where swathes of men are lying,
And horror to shuddering horror crying!
Come home
To the wisdom of those that till the loam,
And give man time for his working-day!

Then the white-blossomed ash will sing—'He cometh,
For whom the loving-cup is poured, the wild bee hummeth.'

* Fifty One Poems (*Cape, 1946*), p. 45.

AN ESTRAY*
(*Chester, 1916*)

How did I come so low,
Wandering here
Under clouds of wrath and woe
With a heart full of fear?

How did I chance to roam
Into the night,
Away from my delicate home
Of colour and light?

Out of a land serene,
Airy and lone,
I strayed to the sadness terrene,
To a people of stone.

Ah, my soul is afraid,
Homesick, estranged.
I long for my palace of jade
And the forest I ranged.

*   * Full version of the poem. The fourth verse
is not included in the version published in* Fifty
One Poems, *p. 59 (*Cape, 1946*).

A CONQUEROR

Cover him swiftly! Cover
The poor stiff hands, the meaningless glazed eyes,
For he, whose nod unmade men's destinies,
Took from the maid her lover,
Sent the red death-fire blazing up the skies—
Is less than a blown leaf on winter days,
And much more helpless than an unborn child.
He, who so seldom smiled,
Now lies with twisted mouth and vacant eyes
Smiling in crazy deprecating-wise
Into death's sinister eyes.
He laid his hand on the beauty that is God,
Leaving it torn and gory.
Hasten then! Hide him in the daisy-sod,
Wrapped in his carrion glory.
Let the blue speedwell light her small lamps over,
And torches of white clover
Burn for the sacrament of life above him,
Who meted death, and died with none to love him.
Let us, in pearl-pale mornings fresh and brave
With new beginnings and with lusty mirth,
Bright with the immortal symbols of the earth,
Send one white moth of prayer to bless his grave—
Pitying, as we grow wiser, more and more,
The man who was so great a conqueror.

HARPS IN HEAVEN

(A Song)

Harps in heaven, made all of glass,
Greener than the rainy grass.
Never one but is bespoken,
And mine is broken, mine is broken!

Harps in heaven play high, play low;
In the cold, rainy wind I go
To find my harp, as green as spring,
My splintered harp, without a string.

FRAGMENTS

There's nothing more to do, she said, and nothing more to say,
For all the wise old Kings are dead, and the lusty lads away.

*

Orion stoops to the lone peak
Like a white crown.
The wind swoops to the larches
In the valley brown.
The dove's note slips from the branches
Softly down.
Like the wind and the star and the song of the dove
Is your love.

THE FLOCKMASTER*

I come
Out of the heart of night, where calm distils
Like dew in the helleborine.
Forever the sheep have known me, straitened and dumb
In their life like a dark ravine;
They clamour of me to the empty sky and the hills;
They cry with a great homesickness under the moon
For something they know and know not, within them, beyond—
That they feel when I dwell on the slope in the heat of noon;
That they taste in the cold dewpond.
Only a little less of me have they known
Than the poet knows, and far as he they have wandered
With their lambs, on the clear skyline like shadows stealing,
Clad in the fleece of their crying,
Following me on whom all creatures have pondered—
Inarticulate, sighing
After the half-revealed, the unrevealing,
The shepherd who dwelleth alone.

* Fifty One Poems, *p*. 61.

Clouds like large brown butterflies
Speeding across the purple downs,
Lifting their pinions above the towns,
Trooped to the east when the first cock crew,
In the steely dew, under steely skies,
And fluttered their wings when the sun came through.

*   *   *   *

The rivers ran from rock to rock
In the old, old hills above,
In the early days of Eden when God,
Unwitting, created love;
Smiled and wondered and pondered long,
And sadly turned to His heaven,
Where silver angels in the golden day
Harped, and no heart was riven.
And that was the time God made the daisies,
And agrimony,
And a brown sedge-warbler to sing His praises
In the pale thorn-tree.
That was the day, in His apple orchard,
He planted the pear,
To chequer the grass with hearted shadows
And fruit like a golden tear.
Yet still, as He dreamed and pondered on earth,
His heart was sad with loss,
And deep in the centre of every blossom
He laid a cross.
The chiming rivers on the granite mountains
In the old, old hills above,
Ran down to the bittersweet valleys, when God,
Unwitting, created love.

Revised poem first written when she was fifteen.

THE THORNLESS ROSE

(A Carol for Peace)

Within our hearts a hundred kings,
   With banners like a silver dove,
And gifts of fair and simple things
   Ride out to meet the lord of love.

Within our hearts new stars have blazed,
   And over moor and mountain all
The sleepy shepherds hear, amazed,
   Songs like an April curlew's call.

Now in a world aghast with tears,
   A new hope burns, a new faith glows,
From the dark fields of bitter years
   At last there springs the thornless rose.

ADAM

What makes a blackbird's song so sweet?
The bitter frost and the sharp sleet.
What gives a poet immortal fame?
Indifference, laughter, a trampled name.

God looked out of his silver house
And saw mankind like a starveling mouse.
He said, 'Should I lift him and take him home
From the black clay and the chill foam,
And smooth away that frown of his
And close his eyes with silences,
He would not draw from the dark mould
Sorrow's fruit of red and gold,
Nor find beneath the bitter sea
Love like a pearl in its purity.'
So he shut the door of his mercies close,
And flung man only a crimson rose.

A young man walked in an orchard apart,
Learning an ancient book by heart,
When a thought crept out of the forest dim
Like a golden snake, and spoke with him
And lipped the book disparagingly,
And said, 'This is but a picture of me.
The poets come, the philosophers come
About me, as bees in the clover hum.
Some write ill, some moderately,
But only the lover has speech of me.
And hark you! Have you, the while you trod
Here in the orchard, talked with God?'
The young man said, 'I have dreamed of him
And heard his step down the ages dim.'
'Give me your book for purchase money
And I will feed you with gall and honey.
You shall see the stuff of life on the loom
And watch God walk in immortal gloom.'

When hearted shadows were multiplied,
And languorous breezes rose and died,
As drawn by magic, a woman came,

Like an apple flower or a white flame.
So thick did the ripe red applies lie,
She trod on them as she wandered by;
Then paused and pondered, pitiful
Of beauty, and gathered with fingers cool
An armful, and came where the young man was.
The snake whispered out of the grass.
She dropped an apple as if by chance
And set her glance to the young man's glance.
He caught her hand, he made her stay,
He took the rosy apples away.
The snake whispered, 'The forest is sweet,
Where pollen finds pollen and lovers meet.'

When to the dark of the forest they came,
She was fuel and he was flame.
To them was given, as they walked therein,
The joy that multitudes die to win.
The meaning of life, as they did lie,
Was to him a shout and to her a sigh.
Freely they stepped, as forth they went,
Stripped of the garments of sentiment.
The glittering snake, as they left the wood,
Said, 'Have you eaten and understood?'
'We have eaten the apple down to the core.'

'Then you are fugitives evermore.'
They gazed on his beauty, afraid, aghast,
And a wailing wind came up and passed.
The serpent softly pillowed his head,
And into a wild rose thicket they fled.

The presence of God was over the trees;
Slowly they bowed, as smoke in the breeze.
The fruit fell down in the quiet day
Like drops of rain from a shaken spray.
And a sigh from every yellowing leaf
Seemed as the voice of a soul in grief.
They heard in their hearts, 'Life is great,
So I give you life, mate with mate.
Come forth!' Then he, triumphant, slim,
Came forth with the zest of life in him,

And forth came she, with soft demur,
The veil of wifehood covering her.
God said, 'I sent you passion, O man!
Like a snake from me to you it ran,
Wild, ruthless, arrogant,
To fire the veins, make the heart pant.
I sent to you, O delicate bride!
Weakness that came like a spring tide.
You shall tread a path you would not go,
And find a miracle wrapped in woe.'
Then God and the serpent were both away
And a cold rain fell at the close of day,
And a blackbird whistled in the trees above,
'Cruelty is the Lord of Love.'

1919

A FACTORY OF PEACE

I watched him in the loud and shadowy lane
Of life; and every face that passed him by
Grew bright and restful, smiling inwardly,
As though he gave for all their grief and pain
Largesse of quiet, soft as summer rain,
And balsam tinctured with tranquillity.
Yet his own eyes were dark with agony.
'O herbalist,' I cried, 'in that calm brain
What tortured thing is moaning while you heal?'
He said—'Where balms are made for human uses,
Red furnace-fires and wheel on grinding wheel
Must crush and purify the crude herb-juices.
Within some hearts the conflict cannot cease:
They are the sick world's factories of peace.'

REFERENCES

I. SHORT STORIES

'A Cedar-Rose', Tales Of Country Life, *Country Life*, July 10, 1909, pp. 47-8.

'Mr. Tallent's Ghost', *The Ghost Book*, ed. Lady Cynthia Asquith (Hutchinson, September 1926), pp. 290-330.

'The Cuckoo Clock', *Sails of Gold*, ed. Lady Cynthia Asquith (Hutchinson, October 1927), pp. 93-105.

'The Sword', *The Cornhill Magazine*, April 1934 (Vol. 149, no. 892), pp. 401-9.

'Glimpses of Old Shropshire', *Transactions Of The Caradoc And Severn Valley Field Club*, Vols. VII and VIII, March 16 1923, pp. 87-93.

   Published in *The Shrewsbury Chronicle* in two parts: 'The Return Of The Romans: A Dream Of Uriconium', March 30 1923; 'Shrewsbury's Abbey Fair', April 6 1923.

The Chinese Lion (Bertram Rota, 1937. Limited Edition of 350 copies).

II. ESSAYS, ARTICLES, REVIEWS

The English Review, 'The Core Of Poetry', February 1920, Vol. 30, pp. 142-4.

T.P's and Cassell's Weekly
   'New Year Customs', December 27 1924, p. 387.
   'Hark How The Birds Do Sing'!, June 27 1925, p. 324.
   'John Halifax Gentleman', April 3 1926, p. 844.
   'The Poetry Of The Prayer Book', April 17 1926, p. 904.

The Daily News
   'A Pedlar Of Leaves', October 30 1924.

The Bookman
   'Morton Luce', June 1925, pp. 148-50.
   'The Soul Of Australia', October 1925, pp. 44-5.
   'Helen Prothero Lewis', November 1925, pp. 111-12.
   'Contrast', April 1926, p. 52.
   ' "Plus Que De L'Esprit" ', May 1926, pp. 130-31.
   'The Wing Of Psyche', July 1926, p. 214.
   'Pilgrims Of Eternity', August 1926, p. 265.
   'A Posy Of Sweet Flowers', September 1926, pp. 300-01.
   ' "Knowest Thou The Land?" ', November 1926, pp. 122-3.
   'One Coming From Calvary', December 1926, pp. 177-8.
   'Our Immortal Jane', February 1927, pp. 256-8.
   'Little Miss Burney', June 1927, pp. 163-4.
   'Irony And Mrs. Wharton', September 1927, p. 303.

The Spectator
    'Birds, Beasts and Trees', December 2 1922, pp. 812-4.
    'Our Birds, Their Haunts And Nests', January 27 1923, p. 152.
    'Birds, Beasts And Flowers', March 24 1923, p. 488.
    'Wild Life In Many Lands', August 11 1923, pp. 194-5.
    'Sense And Sensibility Out Of Doors', October 6 1923, p. 465.
    'When The Pie Was Opened', December 1 1923, p. 856.
    Natural History, December 8 1923, p. 910.
    'Quite Wild Animals', December 22 1923, p. 1002.
    'The Honey Bee', February 9 1924, pp. 207-8.
    'Dabbling In The Dew', March 21 1925, pp. 471-2.
    'The Wayfaring Tree', June 27 1925, p. 1052.
    Other Reviews: Novels of Country Life, December 15 1923; December 29 1923; January 26 1924; February 2 1924.

III. POEMS

Private collections; and in works published by Jonathan Cape Ltd. (see below).

IV. WORKS BY MARY WEBB

The Golden Arrow.
Gone to Earth.
The House in Dormer Forest.
Seven for a Secret.
Precious Bane.
Armour Wherein He Trusted: A Novel and some stories.
Poems And The Spring Of Joy.
The Chinese Lion (Rota).
Fifty One Poems.
A Mary Webb Anthology, edited by Henry B. L. Webb.
The Essential Mary Webb, edited by Martin Armstrong.
Mary Webb: *Selected Poems*, edited, with an Introduction by Gladys Mary Coles.